THE MISUNDERSTOOD JESUS

Ten Lost Keys to Life

Since all our keys are lost or broken,
Shall it be thought absurd
If for an art of words I turn
Discreetly to the Word?
—James McAuley
"An Art of Poetry"

I will give you the keys to the kingdom of heaven, and whatever you bind on earth will be bound in heaven, and whatever you loose on earth will be loosed in heaven.

(Matt 16:19)

THE MISUNDERSTOOD JESUS
Ten Lost Keys to Life

Clyde E. Fant

PEAKE ROAD
Macon, Georgia

ISBN 1-57312-015-4

The Misunderstood Jesus
Ten Lost Keys to Life

Clyde E. Fant

Copyright © 1996
Peake Road

6316 Peake Road
Macon, Georgia 31210-3960
1-800-747-3016

Peake Road
is an imprint of
Smyth & Helwys Publishing, Inc.®

All rights reserved.
Printed in the United States of America.

The paper used in this publication meets the minimum
requirements of American Standard for Information
Sciences—Permanence of Paper for Printed Library Material.
ANSI Z39.48–1984.

Library of Congress Cataloging-in-Publication Data

Fant, Clyde E.
    The misunderstood Jesus: ten lost keys to life/
by Clyde E. Fant.
    x + 166 pp.   6" x 9" (15 x 23 cm.)
    ISBN 1-573312-015-4
    1. Jesus Christ—Teachings I. Title.
    BS2415.F36   1996
    232.9'54—dc20   94-41134
                                                                     CIP

CONTENTS

Preface vii

Acknowledgments ix

Chapter 1
   Sanity: The Word Turned Upside Down 1

Chapter 2
   Grace: The Robe of the Prodigal 12

Chapter 3
   Law: From Psalmist's Delight to Puritan's Despair 28

Chapter 4
   The Self: The Fantasy Child and the "Real Me" 51

Chapter 5
   Wealth: When Life Is Rich 68

Chapter 6
   Meekness: The Bold Shall Inherit the Freeways 89

Chapter 7
   Anger: The Cycle of Vengeance and the Circle of Love 104

Chapter 8
   Contentment: Burnout and the Thirty-Percent Solution 122

Chapter 9
   Sympathy: The Alien Becomes Family 135

Chapter 10
   Touch: The Hands of Jesus 152

For
Brian, Carol, and Julie
Jonathan, Preston, and Emily
My children and grandchildren

Preface

Is Jesus misunderstood? This book says he is. But if so, how, and why?

It wasn't long after the death of Jesus that virtually everyone began putting their own interpretations on his teachings. Even the New Testament shows signs of that. And the church of the early centuries mostly used his radical concepts as pastel tints to be stirred into the buckets of their own cultural paint. No surprise, then, that the church's redo of its world, both civic and private, mostly resembled the tastes of secular society.

It's still happening. Sayings of Jesus have been used to portray him as everything from a flower-power hippy to a power-lurch capitalist. Scholars make him a wandering Stoic philosopher, a Jewish magician, or an apocalyptic visionary. Churches bend him left and right, activist and passivist, pro-life and pro-choice. Mega-churches seek to dominate their towns in his name, while sectarian groups seek refuge in the isolation of a culture from a remote age.

Churches aren't alone in this attempt to carve the meaning of life in their own image. Everybody out there thinks they've got the key or meaning to life. On a recent bookstore trip I counted one aisle for religion, three for New Age, and six for self-help. (Fiction had ten aisles, unless you count New Age and self-help; then it had nineteen.)

The point of this book is simple. I believe Jesus gave the church the answers to life. Sometimes the church gets mixed-up about what he meant. Then the keys are lost to everybody, church and nonchurch alike. That's not good.

I don't think this book names all the keys to the Kingdom. It certainly doesn't say all that could be said about them. In some places, no doubt, it's even wrong. (I don't know where; if I did, I'd fix it.) But I'm sure these ten chapters talk about keys to life. I'm also sure Jesus knew how to use them to unlock the meaning of life. And I know, at times, the church—that's us—has lost them, or at least misplaced them.

Once Daniel Boone was asked if he had ever gotten lost. He thought a minute, then said: "Lost? No, I never was lost. But I was bewildered once for three days." If this is a time when some of these keys seem to be misplaced, I hope this book can point us in their general direction.

One other word. We shouldn't get smug about who Jesus was and what we know about him. If we do, we too are on a sure-fire route to misunderstanding him. Jesus won't sit meekly on our stage like a famous but senile professor while his latest *Wunderkind* speaks for him. In *Finally Comes the Poet,* Walter Bruggemann quotes Andrew Greely on "the real Jesus":

> The only real Jesus is one who is larger than life, who escapes our categories, who eludes our attempts to reduce Him for our cause. Any Jesus who has been made to fit our formula ceases to be appealing precisely because He is no longer wondrous, mysterious, surprising. We may reduce Him to a right-wing Republican conservative or a gun-toting Marxist revolutionary and thus rationalize and justify our own political ideology. But having done so, we are dismayed to discover that whoever we have signed on as an ally is not Jesus. Categorize Jesus and He isn't Jesus anymore.

If we can hear Jesus against ourselves, as well as for ourselves, we may discover the "real Jesus," the one who points us to the true meaning of life.

I've dedicated this book to my children and their children. That says how important I think all of this is.

Acknowledgments

Thanks

— to Stetson University for the sabbatical leave to get started on this project
— to Tessa Immich, who labored through the countless rewrites and put it all together
— to the many friends, too many to name, who listened (sometimes willingly) and made suggestions
— to my wife, Cheryl Hammock, who saw a lot of things about these keys I didn't
— to my mother, Margaret Fant, who likes everything I write, even the parts she hasn't read
— to Smyth and Helwys for publishing this book

Chapter 1

SANITY
The Word Turned Upside Down

If we're going to look for the meanings to life, shouldn't we begin at a better place than sanity? I mean, since we're all inmates of the same asylum, how would any of us know when we found it, this lost key to sanity? Wouldn't someone have to tell us what is truly sane and what passes for sane but is truly insane? How would we know the difference? That's the problem. We can only define sanity by comparing what all of us do and declaring sane those things most of us do. Insanity is what the rest of us do—which sometimes gets the whole thing reversed.

Take Vincent van Gogh, for instance. Did you know he began his life as a missionary? Really. "He has sent me to preach the gospel to the poor," Vincent wrote to his brother Theo in 1876. Apparently he did a good job of it, too. But he took it so seriously that he gave away all of his possessions, including most of his clothes, to the impoverished Belgian coal-miners who were his smutty flock. So the Dutch Reformed Church decided he was insane and gave him the boot from his mission. Anyway, Vincent decided he and Jesus knew who the crazy ones really were, and in 1879 he left the church.

But as disillusioned as Van Gogh was with the church, his faith in God was as strong as ever. He threw himself into his art with the same zeal he had devoted to his mission. He called his work as an artist, "walking with God." Van Gogh continued to believe that God urges all people to love with reckless abandon. So, thanks to the sane and sober thinking of the Dutch Reformed Church, this crazy world lost a great missionary but gained a great painter.

You'd think the church would eventually learn. The church of Rome had already done the same thing to Francesco Bernadone when he resolved to serve the poor; renounced his father's wealth; and stripped himself naked as a jaybird before his father, his bishop, God, and a crowd of popeyed neighbors. All but God declared him crazy on the spot. That was in 1206. Twenty years later he was dead. And two years after that, the church decided that this crazy man who had spent his brief life caring for beggars and lepers was really a saint—Saint Francis of Assisi.

So maybe there was a touch of madness—or maybe more than a touch—in Vincent van Gogh or, for that matter, in Francesco Bernadone. But it sure wasn't when they gave their lives to the poor and helpless. How do we get so turned around about what makes sense and what is crazy? All of us, even church-going folks? (Sometimes especially church-going folks.)

We are the victims of misdirection, of faulty compasses. We have been told by our culture that up is down, black is white, ignorance is bliss, guns don't kill people, he who dies with the most toys wins, and God only knows what else. We're not sure anymore whether we should put our hat on our feet or our milk in the oven. Not knowing who you are or where you are in this spinning world can be fatal. Garrison Keillor, one of the sane among us, wrote these words:

> My poor great-grandpa, when his house burned down when Grandma left the bread baking in the summer kitchen oven to go visit the Berges and they built the new one facing west instead of south: they say he was confused the rest of his life and never got straightened out even when he set up his bed in the parlor (which faced north as his former bedroom had): he lived in a twilight world for some time and then moved in his mind to the house he'd grown up in, and in the end didn't know one day from another until the day he died. "Yea, though I walk through the valley of the shadow of death, I will fear no evil," but there's more than one kind of shadow, and when a man loses track, it can kill him. Nothing could have saved my great-grandpa. He died of misdirection.[1]

The Bible and Insanity

The writings that both Jews and Christians call scripture take a surprising interest in the subject of sanity. Once when David was running for his life from King Saul, he feigned madness before his enemies, clawed the door frame with his fingernails, and drooled and dribbled spit into his beard. The king of Gath, who must have had a pretty good sense of humor, asked his servants (more or less), "Why have you brought this crazy man to me? Am I short of madmen around here, so you have to bring a genuine loony to entertain me? You're not bringing him into my house" (proving, as it turned out, that neither he nor David was crazy). (1 Sam 21:3)

In the book of Daniel we're told how God drove King Nebuchadnezzar out of human society because he thought he was bigger than God. Like most people when they are cut off from human contact, Nebuchadnezzar lost his sanity. Only in his case, the effects were definitely worse than average. He ate grass like an ox and lived among the animals, creeping around among their hooves. The dew wet his back every night, and his hair grew as long as eagles' feathers and his fingernails as long as birds' claws.

Nebuchadnezzar lived like an animal until he learned that the Most High (what he called God after that) actually rules over earthly kingdoms no matter who sits on the throne. Once he figured that out, his reason returned to him, and he stood up on his hind legs like a human being, spit the grass out of his mouth, and praised and honored God. But it was only after he "lifted his eyes to heaven" that his reason returned to him. This should be a hint, I guess, to all of us who run businesses or offices, or whatever we do that makes us think we're in charge of the world, about the difference between a sane understanding of life and living like an animal.

The New Testament also describes tales of sanity and insanity. When that strange ascetic, John the Baptizer, began dunking perfectly respectable Jewish people underwater, wearing goat hides, and, most of all, abstaining from the rich foods and drinks of his neighbors, everybody knew he was crazy. "He has a devil," was the less-than-tactful way they put it. Of course, Jesus' contrary evaluation was that there never was a greater person than John. Then, because Jesus enjoyed what few wedding parties and the like he was invited to, they called him a glutton and a sot—thereby proving that when somebody really despises you, they'll call you crazy whatever you do.

Later, when the apostle Paul stood before the Roman governor, Festus, and told him more than he wanted to know about the ways of God, Festus said, "You've read too many books, Paul; it's turned you into a maniac!" (Acts 26:24, my translation). Sanity for Festus, as for most people who have a good thing, consisted mainly in leaving well-enough alone and not rocking his own canoe. Of course, Paul and all the other early Christians were regarded as crazy people by their neighbors because they tried to live like Jesus. And Jesus' idea of life was so different from that of everybody else that even his own family at times thought he was seriously insane.

Once when Jesus was teaching, his mother and brothers came out to seize him—forcibly if they had to—and take him home. Reports had gotten back to them of how upset the pious folk were with Jesus because of the strange things he was saying. There were ugly rumors that he was out of his head. His family wanted to take him back to the family carpentry shop and the obscure life. He could still turn out a good table or a chair; he didn't have to be ridiculed and mocked, even if he was more than a little strange. When Jesus learned that his family was there to take him home, he cried out in frustration and disappointment: "Who is my mother, and who are my kinfolks? Those who are in this thing with me!" (Matt 12:48, my translation.) Apparently, sanity—like beauty—is in the eye of the beholder.

What Is Normal?

Modern psychology doesn't use the terms "sanity" and "insanity" very often. These words are generally used only in legal definitions, where they apply to whether somebody knows right from wrong. Psychology more often speaks of normality and abnormality, even though it still has a hard time saying what these terms mean. One psychology text defines normality, or emotional well-being, by these six qualities:

(1) Normal people have an efficient perception of reality. Well adjusted people are generally realistic in knowing their capabilities and reactions and in interpreting what's happening in the world about them.

(2) Normal people possess self-knowledge. People who are well-adjusted have some awareness of their own feelings and motives in what they do.

(3) Normal people have the ability to exercise voluntary control over their behavior. Individuals who are emotionally well-adjusted can usually control their reactions in a variety of situations.

(4) Normal people feel self-esteem and acceptance. Well-adjusted people have some sense of their own self-worth and generally feel accepted by those around them.

(5) Normal people have the ability to form affectionate relationships. Individuals who are emotionally well-adjusted are able to form close and satisfying relationships with other people.

(6) Normal people lead productive lives. Well-adjusted individuals are able to direct their energies into efforts that are productive for themselves and society.²

At first glance, these characterizations of normalcy only seem to reinforce the distance between our century and the first century. Who, in the time of Jesus, had such an understanding of "normal" or of "emotional well-being"? Granted, those weren't the favorite campfire topics of Jesus and his disciples. They never came to him to ask, "Lord, why couldn't we define 'normal' to our group?" And he never said, "Seek ye first emotional well-being, and all these things will be added to you." But in some of his experiences, Jesus seemed intent on restoring troubled people to a state of well-being. Take, for example, the strange case of the man in the tombs (Matt 8; Mark 5; Luke 8).

The Mad Man of Gerasa

Jesus crossed the Sea of Galilee with his disciples and immediately encountered a man who was clearly abnormal by anybody's definition. He was buck-naked and howling mad. He smacked himself with rocks, slung around the chains the normal folks tried to subdue him with, and generally scared the daylights out of everybody. The good townspeople had long ago given up the idea of chaining and guarding him. The man had maniacal strength. So they drove him out of town, out to the tombs where nobody in their right mind would live. There he stayed—homeless, crazy, and in bad need of help.

As soon as Jesus set foot out of the boat, the madman howled and made a rush at him, which probably caused a general panic among the sober sorts who were his disciples. Jesus, however, stood his ground. The "Gadarene demoniac," as the King James Version rather poetically put it, then stuck his face in Jesus' face, his eyes wide and wild. "Leave me alone," he howled, "do not destroy me!" "Who are you?" Jesus asked. "What is your name?" "I am Legion," he cried (in the words of the good KJV), "because many devils were entered into him" (Luke 8:30).

Even modern psychology can't quarrel very much with that evaluation, even if it sees his demons somewhat differently. After all, the man flunked the sanity test on all six counts:

(1) He definitely didn't have an efficient perception of reality (to put it mildly).
(2) He had no self-knowledge. He had no idea what he was doing or why he was doing it.
(3) He obviously couldn't exercise voluntary control over his behavior. In fact, he couldn't be controlled involuntary, with chains.
(4) He had no self-esteem or self-acceptance. When asked his name, his ego was so impaired that he didn't see himself as one person, or even one demon. He was Legion (the term for the Roman army unit of 6,000 troops), a fragmented and shattered self.
(5) He sure couldn't form affectionate relationships. God only knows how long it had been since another human being had hugged him, or even touched him, except to hit him and drive him away.
(6) And productive? His life? Is it productive to beat your body black and blue with stones, as he did in his torment and self-loathing?

No, by our modern definitions this man was definitely abnormal and anything but well-adjusted. Actually, he was in serious trouble even according to the ancient definition of madness in the Jewish Talmud. The popular definition of madness in that day included four characteristics: tearing one's clothes, walking abroad at night, spending a night on a grave, and destroying what one was given. This man definitely fit the picture. He had ripped off his clothes, lived in tombs day and night, and destroyed everything anybody had given him—which, up until now, consisted solely of a large set of chains. They also had given him a lot of grief. (He really was grieving, you know, along with all his rage, grieving for his lost self.)

No wonder the good citizens of Gadara, or Gerasa, or wherever he was from, decided enough was enough! But nothing they did worked, neither controlling him with chains nor isolating him in tombs, which was sort of the first-century equivalent of our ghettoes. Meanwhile, he became more and more destructive to himself and to society. (By the way, if you start getting any mental images of our society and its shabby attempts to deal with the mentally ill—now mostly turned out into the streets—or the homeless, the inner-city poor, or what-have-you, it's no coincidence.)

Then this strange story comes to its even stranger, unpredictable end. Jesus drove the evil spirits from the man's mind, and they entered into a herd of swine. The pigs then rushed into the abyss, the depths of the sea, which people in that time believed to be the original habitation of demons. With the fragmentation of his self gone, the man next appeared before the townspeople "clothed" and "in his right mind."

In the ancient adoption formulas of that time, the new parents of an orphan said, "I have clothed him." It was an expression of their acceptance of the child and their commitment to care for him. Clothing was one of the principal forms of wealth in the ancient world. To clothe someone was to indicate your willingness to share your means with them as a member of the family.

This wild man of Gerasa appears at the end of the story "clothed" —again a member of the human family—and "in his right mind"— with personal wholeness. What chains could not do, compassion had done. The man was found sitting quietly at the feet of Jesus, at one with himself and with society. Of course, his neighbors were shocked, to say the least, and the loss of their pigs weighed far heavier on their minds than the cure of one bizarre local character. Furthermore, they were scared to death to find out that this Jewish healer had power upon their Gentile shores. (They raised pigs, unclean to Jews; they had to be Gentiles.) So they urged Jesus to go away and take his economy-damaging powers with him.

The healed man then begged Jesus to let him go along with him in his travels. But Jesus told him to return to his own city and tell his neighbors what God had done. And so he did, to the amazement of everybody who heard his story or saw the sane and gentle spirit of the former freak, the wild man from Gerasa.

A nice story, a good ending. But so what? What sense can we make out of such a strange and ancient episode? What can it tell us about our own brand of craziness?

The Shadow-Side

All stories of demonic possession in the New Testament are intended to reveal the distortion and destruction of the image of God in humankind. The more destroyed this image, the more monstrous the distorted person. What the ancients saw as demonic, of course, we might tend to see as evil, either natural evil such as mental illness or spiritual evil such as deliberate criminality. However we define it, it's obvious that the demonic is alive and well in our society—and, as much as we try to ignore it, even in ourselves.

It's unnerving that sometimes we catch a glimpse of a darkness in us we don't know how to name. Carl Jung, one of the founding figures of modern psychology, wrote:

> It is a frightening thought that man [sic] also has a shadow-side to him, consisting not just of little weaknesses and foibles, but of a positively demonic dynamism. The individual seldom knows anything of this; to him as an individual it is incredible that he should ever in any circumstances go beyond himself. But let these harmless creatures form a mass, and there emerges a raging monster; and each individual is only one tiny cell in the monster's body, so that for better or worse he must accompany it on its bloody rampages and even assist it to the utmost. Having a dark suspicion of these grim possibilities, man turns a blind eye to the shadow-side of human nature. Blindly he strives against the salutary dogma of original sin, which is yet so prodigiously true. Yes, he even hesitates to admit the conflict of which he is so painfully aware.[3]

The events of recent years have forced us to look at our shadow-side, like it or not. We have learned that we are capable of a frightening insanity, even the best educated of us. Like the pig owners in the story, we believe life must run according to our needs, our formulas for usefulness. People must serve our economic and social interests, or we want to banish them—or worse.

If you drive on the Autobahn in Germany from Stuttgart to Munich, eventually you'll see a large exit sign with just two names on it. If you turn north, you'll reach one town; if you turn south, you'll reach the other. By a grimly ironic coincidence, the two names on the sign are Dachau and Festenfeldbruck. Doesn't mean anything to you? It was at Festenfeldbruck that German soldiers risked their lives in an attempt to rescue the Israeli Olympic team held hostage by terrorists. But it was at Dachau, just a few miles up the road, that thousands of Jews were killed in the gas chambers and ovens by Nazi Germans under Hitler's rule. On the same road, in one direction heroic sacrifice; in the other, demonic slaughter. And people of the same country did both. It is a parable of the world's insanity.

The shadow-side of us, as Jung put it, is frighteningly real and ever-present. Sometimes we sense it when we catch ourselves grinning at the tears of someone we dislike, or when we con somebody into a deal, or when we cheat on something or someone. But we don't look at that side of us for long. That's the way life is, we say; I'm no worse than anybody else. True. And no better, either. Most of us suffer from a case of misplaced moral superiority.

If we think that only Nazi Germans or Imperial Japanese could commit the atrocities of Dachau or Corregidor, we must have forgotten My Lai in the Vietnam War. But I won't soon forget the fresh-faced, handsome, blond, crew-cut, belligerent veteran in the parking lot of a mall in Little Rock, Arkansas. It was shortly after Lieutenant Calley had been charged in the massacre at My Lai. The veteran was collecting signatures on a petition to free Calley. He was livid with rage at my refusal to excuse the same conduct we had so roundly damned in our enemies in World War II.

When we want something badly enough, when our closest interests are at risk, all of us are capable of making sanity out of insanity. And insanity is much worse collectively than individually. It's hard to see that. We know the insanity of the would-be Napoleon on the grounds of the sanitarium, but it's harder to recognize the insanity of the real Napoleons of commerce or politics or business. We see the horror of the serial killer and the mass murderer. Yet we tolerate, and even excuse, the economic and social tyranny that cripples and kills whole races and nations. After all, business is business.

These days we are also seeing the insanity of the violation of our beautiful blue planet. Virtually every element of creation is under assault, from air to water to earth to creatures, from rain forests to mountain streams, from great silverback gorillas and black rhinos in Africa to tiny key deer and scrubjays in Florida. Some of this loss is through carelessness; the worst is through wantonness. In our greed, we act as though humans own the earth in fee simple. When we destroy part of it, we forget we are destroying part of ourselves. Erazim Kohak wrote,

> Emanuel Radl recounts the story of the Spanish anatomist Vesalius, condemned to make a pilgrimage to the Holy Land after a supposed corpse he was dissecting opened its eyes and stared at the audience in agony. Radl writes, "What if the cosmos were to raise its head, stare at us and cry out, 'People, what are you doing to me?'—To what Holy Land would we then travel in a hair shirt to beg forgiveness?"[4]

But the cosmos cannot speak. Like the silent animals that accompany us through life, creation can only stare mutely at the perceiving, reflecting creature that walks on two legs beside it through time. Paul voiced its hopes best: "For the creation waits with eager longing for the revealing of the children of God." And later, "We know that the whole creation has been groaning . . . until now" (Rom 8:19, 22). It is up to us to see more than the comptroller's bottom line, more than the corporation's return on equity, more than the insanity of a dollars-only cost-and-feasibility study of life. We must see the divine gift in nature, the eternal in the least of creation. Kohak perceives this as humanity's highest calling:

> Certainly, humans can become wholly absorbed in the preoccupations of time. As there are humans who are color-blind, so there can be humans who become blind to goodness, to truth and beauty, who drink wine without pausing to cherish it, who pluck flowers without pausing to give thanks, who accept joy and grief as all in a day's work, to be enjoyed or managed, without ever seeing the presence of eternity in them. But that is not the point. . . . Were it not for humans who are able to see it, to grieve for it and to cherish it, the goodness, beauty, and truth of creation would remain wholly absorbed in the passage of time and pass with it. It is our calling to inscribe it into eternity.[5]

The grim fact is, the shadow-side of human existence is not only dark and real. It is also enormous. Looming above each of us individually and all of us collectively, the dark side of human endeavor, the insane side, threatens our very existence as a human race. What can the strange story of a possessed man and a mysterious healer do about that? It can point us all toward sanity, one of our lost meanings to life.

Where Is Sanity?
For Jesus, sanity is only where the will of God is done. Even among the classic Greeks, insanity was always understood as wherever the ways of the gods and humankind part. That's how Jesus understood it, too. Wherever humankind departs from the ways of God, insanity begins.

This story of a possessed man is told in the Gospels as evidence of the in-breaking of the reign of God and its liberation of us all from insanity. Surprisingly, according to this story, Jesus had authority even in Gentile, foreign territory. That was no small thing in a world that believed new gods waited like customs inspectors every time anybody crossed a border. With the coming of Jesus, this story says, the liberation of God knows no boundaries. Even a pagan madman can receive the grace of God. So this experience of Jesus points us to two great truths: Jesus can cure us of our craziness, and Jesus can cure *any* of us of our craziness.

But Christ's way looked insane then, and it looks insane now. "These are the ones who have turned the world upside down," they complained of the first-century followers of Christ. (Acts 17:6) What is clearly sane to us, the worldly wise-types said, is insane to them; and what is sane to them, we know for sure is insane. After all, they said, look at how well we are dressed, and look at how badly they are dressed! Look at what we have, and look at what they have. If they're so right and righteous, why ain't they rich? Does anybody doubt who's smart and who's crazy, or who's blessed by the gods?

The way of Jesus does turn the world upside down. But that's only because it was standing on its head in the first place. God has not arbitrarily ruled one way of life to be right and another wrong. God has revealed through the gospel the way things are. Under the reign of God, power and tyranny, greed and cruelty are deposed, and the weak, the old, the ill, the poor, the child, the woman, and the foreigner are no longer beneath dignity but favored in the eyes of God.

To live according to God's truth about life and human beings is sanity. To live contrary to that truth is insanity. That is why sanity is the first of the lost keys to life. To understand life as mirrored in the actions of Jesus of Nazareth is to find a key that unlocks the door to life—real life—where every human being may grow and flourish, and where all creatures and creation are cared for as a gift from God. That world makes sense. That life is sanity. Behind the other door is bedlam.

Notes

[1] Garrison Keillor, *Lake Wobegon Days* (New York: Penguin Books, 1986) 178-79.

[2] Rita L. Atkinson, Richard G. Atkinson, Edward E. Smith, Ernest R. Hilgard, *Introduction to Psychology* (New York: Harcourt, Brace, Jovanovich, 1987) 490-91.

[3] Carl Gustav Jung, "Acknowledging Your Shadow-Side" in *Two Essays on Analytical Psychology*, trans. R. F. C. Hull, vol. 7 of *Collected Works*, 2nd. ed. (New York: Pantheon, 1966) 30.

[4] Erazim Kohak, *The Embers and the Stars* (Chicago: The University of Chicago Press) 236.

[5] Ibid., 84-85.

Chapter 2

GRACE

The Robe of the Prodigal

"Do your best," they said to us as they sent us out the door. And where were we then? We weren't sure. But there we stood, favored children, at the door of the first grade—or was it college? Anyhow, it was life, and it was real. We stood there, armed by the love of our parents, with their farewell kisses still wet on our cheeks. "Do your best," they said.

So why did that depress us, if ever so slightly? Why, in the sunshine of their loving favor—with the high hopes not only of ourselves and our parents but of all the generations of our elders ringing in our ears—why did that gray fog of depression swirl about us, if only for a moment? Could it be that we somehow sensed that our journey to the promised land might turn instead into forty years of wilderness wandering? That the ecstacy of anticipation might turn into the agony of defeat? That "do your best" might come to mean half-exhausted, sometimes half-hearted efforts at life? Or that it might become a millstone of guilt about our necks rather than wings for our feet?

So, too, God kissed Israel and sent it out into the world, a favored child. In innocence it began, with the promises to Abraham of a child that would lead to a mighty nation as numerous as the sands of the shore or the stars in the sky. The experience was one of ecstacy at the beginning, as it is for all delighted parents and children, and none of the agony—for a while.

It was Christmas, and the K-Mart store was filled with the usual last-minute shoppers. A huge man pushed a shopping cart slowly down the crowded aisles. Nestled in its upper reaches was a baby, so tiny it could not have been more than a few days old. Bundled and wrapped securely against even the mild December weather of Florida, only its small face showed.

The man looked out of place. Even in the democratic quarters of a K-Mart store, he looked as if he belonged in a less refined setting— a biker bar, for instance. He was enormous, with a red plaid flannel shirt that made him look all the larger buttoned just under his bushy black beard. His turned-up sleeves showed dragon tatoos on both forearms. His face was wide, and his features were large. His ears stood out like microwave relay dishes on either side of his head. His face looked like an old Studebaker coming down the street with both doors open.

But as he shopped he talked constantly to his tiny little boy, leaning across the shopping cart and stroking the baby's cheek with one huge finger. He talked and cooed to the baby, as best a 300-pound man can coo. He scarcely could take his eyes off the baby long enough to find things on the shelves. Everyone smiled at him, but he was oblivious to the crowds. Whatever else he was, he was madly in love with that child. Whatever the future meant to him, most of it was in that baby. And whereas the father was huge, dark, shaggy, and tattooed and whereas the baby was tiny, fair, smooth, and unblemished . . . but he had his father's ears.

So Israel began, new and fresh and hopeful. Yet we are all "flesh of our flesh," and someday, we know, the tiny child in the shopping cart will resemble its parent in more ways than just the Studebaker-door ears. "Do your best," we were told, and so was Israel.

The marquee on the Bible read, "The Agony and the Ecstacy," and Mr. and Mrs. Israel decided to go in and see the show.

"I think I've seen this. Isn't this about the life of Michelangelo, or Vincent van Gogh, or somebody?" Mrs. Israel said. "It certainly sounds familiar."

"Who knows?" Mr. Israel said. "I think it's one of those biblical epics, maybe with Charlton Heston. Anyway, let's see it."

First the "Preview of Coming Attractions" played. "Genesis!" flashed on the screen. "Never before anything like it!"

"Well, I should hope not," murmured Mr. Israel.

"The story of a young couple struggling to make their way in a new world!" the caption read. "It was Paradise—until the Serpent came!" Scenes of Paradise rapidly followed: flowering trees and blue waterfalls.

"This is the 'Ecstacy' part," Mrs. Israel whispered. "I just hope it doesn't turn out to be a horror movie, with that snake thing."

Then brief scenes of the family followed: two children, both boys.

"A boy and a girl would have been nicer," Mrs. Israel whispered.

"Hush!" Mr. Israel said, "or they'll throw us out of here!"

"But when they can't keep even the simple rules of the Garden," the voice-over cries, "they are expelled from Paradise! And the first murderer is born!"

Quick scenes of a bloody struggle follow. Cain kills Abel. A mark appears on his forehead, and he sadly turns and walks away.

"This looks good!" Mr. Israel says. "I think I want to see more of this."

"I'm afraid we will," Mrs. Israel murmurs.

The main feature begins, and they are caught up in the saga of Abraham's journey, Israel in Egypt, Israel fleeing Egypt through the sea and crossing the desert.

"Is that Charlton Heston?" Mrs. Israel asks.

"Don't be silly, that's Moses!" Mr. Israel says.

"Well, who knew?" Mrs. Israel says.

After the movie, they are both outside once again. They are subdued.

"Did you like it?" Mrs. Israel says. "I don't know if I liked it. I liked the burning bush part and the Red Sea part, but I didn't like the ending when Moses died."

"I know," Mr. Israel says. "That was too sad. But the adventure parts were good, and Israel did make it to the Promised Land. I agree with you, though. If they change that ending, more people will come to see it." They leave.

Grace Old and New

"Do your best," God said to Israel. But Israel, like us, didn't always do its best. Israel was favored, but also flawed (Isa 63:7-10). If Israel had been measured strictly according to its laws, it never would have made it to the Promised Land. The agony of the story of Israel was its human failures. The ecstacy of the story of Israel was not its experience of paradise, but its experience of grace. When Israel was most broken and despairing and hopeless, the lovingkindness of God *(chesed)*, God's merciful grace, was given again and again.

Grace is not a new concept in the New Testament. From the journeys of Abraham to the wanderings of the children of Israel, from the sins of Moses to the sins of David, the story of the family of Israel is eminently a story of grace. In the Hebrew Scriptures the actions of

Grace

Yahweh repeatedly made plain God's willingness to forgive wayward Israel. Likewise, the words of the prophets, from Amos to Isaiah to Malachi, make clear the prominent place of little people, the widows, the poor, and the outcast. Those who believe that the Old Testament is a story of law and the New Testament is a story of grace have overlooked the central message of every Old Testament story. Even the book of Leviticus is about the meaning of grace.[1]

We were humans from the beginning: favored but flawed. Our attempts to "do our best" as brothers and sisters to one another, and to serve as caretakers of God's beautiful creation, soon broke down into struggles for pre-eminence and power. But still we were God's children. So God dealt with us with justice, but justice tempered by grace. Because grace was God's nature from the beginning, grace was God's plan from the beginning. That was not always understood by every actor in the Old Testament story. Yet grace alone made possible God's blessings in the Old Testament, just as in the New. The same God who was the loving parent of Jesus Christ was also the parent of Abraham, Isaac, and Jacob, of Sarah, Rebecca, and Leah.

By the New Testament era, however, for most people the key to grace had been lost, buried under the mountains of religious and political intrigues of the past four centuries. God's lovingkindness had been buried deep under the Jerusalem bureaucracy, the legalistic wranglings of religious parties, and the cynicism of the Roman-controlled high priesthood that had been bought and sold for years under foreign domination. Greed and revenge became active players in Israel's religious struggles. The aristocracy controlled the high priesthood and the temple, providing, of course, that they did not arouse the ire of Rome. The common people increasingly found themselves at odds with this hierarchy that mockingly referred to them as "people of the land," those whose daily labors made it impossible for them to follow the myriad rules of cleanliness and scrupulosity of the religious establishment.

Nevertheless, when foreign rulers squeezed Israel's hierarchy for money, they in turn squeezed the people. The peasant class in Israel, to which Jesus belonged, resented the aristocracy and its high-living and high-handed treatment. Galilee was notorious for such feelings. But actually Judea, surrounding Jerusalem, was more of a hotbed of rebellion than Galilee. Finally, in the years 63–66 A.D., thirty years after the death of Jesus, the peasants launched an all-out war against the aristocracy and the temple establishment. Only the crushing power of Rome finally settled the argument. It annihilated the Jewish state in 70 A.D., leveling the temple and destroying the priesthood forever. Only the synagogues and rabbis of the countryside survived.

According to Luke 4, when Jesus began his ministry, these events lay far away. He was invited to speak in his home synagogue in Nazareth, a small obscure village of Galilee not mentioned in the Old Testament. Such invitations were common in first-century synagogues; any Jewish man might be invited to speak. Only his neighbors were there to hear him. But this speech was no common Sabbath sermon. It was to reveal the direction, the trajectory, of Jesus' ministry.

As was their custom in the synagogue, Jesus stood to read his text and sat down to interpret it. The scroll of the prophet Isaiah was given to him, and he unrolled it and read these words in Isaiah 61:1-2:

> The Spirit of the Lord is upon me, bcause he has anointed me to bring good news to the poor. He has sent me to proclaim release to the captives and recovery of sight to the blind, To let the oppressed go free, to proclaim the year of the Lord's favor.

Our Grace: Not Yours

After Jesus read the Isaiah passage, he rolled up the scroll, handed it back to the synagogue attendant, and sat down. And "the eyes of all in the synagogue were fixed on him" (Luke 4:20). Jesus said, "Today this scripture has been fulfilled in your hearing" (v. 21). It was a good beginning. The listeners nodded in agreement, hearing what they wished to hear. What an impressive speaker! they said. "Is this not Joseph's son?" They were amazed at such "gracious words" from a neighbor's boy, and a carpenter's son at that.

But the material he was handling was explosive, much more so than they could imagine. His text referred to the year of Jubilee (Exod 23:10-11; Lev 25:8-17, 23-55; 27:16-25; Deut 15:1-18). The notion of a Jubilee year was an amazing concept. Without question it stands as the most radical piece of social legislation ever prescribed by any nation. Under this law certain events were to take place in the Jubilee year, the fiftieth year occurring at the end of seven sabbatical cycles of seven years each. All land was to be returned to its ancestral owner, all Israelite slaves were to be freed, and all debts were to be forgiven ("Every creditor shall remit the claim that is held against a neighbor"

[Deut 15:2]). Furthermore, they were commanded to lend to the poor even though the Jubilee year was approaching.

> Be careful that you do not entertain a mean thought, thinking, "The seventh year, the year of remission, is near," and therefore view your needy neighbor with hostility and give nothing; your neighbor might cry to the Lord against you, and you would incur guilt. (v. 9)

The land was to remain idle, and all fruit or grain that might grow spontaneously on it was to be left to the poor and the animals.

So why did Jesus' neighbors become so enraged if this piece of social legislation was long established in the Law? First, because he said, "Today this is fulfilled in your ears." Paradise had begun. The inequities of land-grabbing were to be corrected and debts were to be forgiven. The land was Yahweh's. Of course, Jesus' listeners were aware that the land always had belonged to God. Jesus declared, however, that the time had come for each person, no matter how poor or how weak, to receive his just portion of the Promised Land.

Remember that this message was delivered to Galileans, for whom the land was precious above everything. They cared little for the temple establishment, and the subtleties of the Law as propounded by the scribes were a matter of indifference to most of them. But land—that was different. They were farmers, and nothing was more sacred to them than the Promised Land (or the promised acreage). Those who had received more of it had no interest in relinquishing even one foot of land to rectify any social injustices. After all, the Jubilee year was mostly understood as a symbolic price of legislation, an ideal. Whether it was ever practiced in Israel is questionable. Besides, such radical land reform and lending practices were not practical in a modern state such as Israel in the first century. "Paradise" would simply have to be postponed.

Jesus' neighbors were also angered by two well-known stories from their history that Jesus told. Previously they had never gotten the point of them, certainly not as Jesus told them. (Few in our churches today have gotten it, either.) The first story told of the journey of Elijah to Sidon in Phoenicia during a severe famine over the region. There he was cared for by a widow, even though she had meal and oil enough for only one last meal for herself and her son. Elijah promised that their oil and meal would not fail, according to the promise of

God, until the drought ended and rain fell again on the earth. So they all were sustained by the hand of God for many days.

The story sounds innocent enough on the surface. Why did it so enrage the congregation in the synagogue? Jesus made the point that at the time Elijah was sent to Sidon in Phoenicia, a foreign country and the hometown of Jezebel (daughter of Ethbaal, king of Sidon), Israel was full of widows. Yet God sent Elijah to none of them. Elijah, who previously had been cared for in Israel only by ravens in the wilderness, was cared for in Phoenicia by a "heathen" woman in the hometown of Jezebel, the despised enemy of Elijah (and Israel). As a result of Israel's indifference, this foreign widow alone was sustained by Elijah, presumably while widows in Israel starved.

Now is it apparent why the Nazareth congregation was angry? Imagine an American preacher at the height of the Cold War telling a similar story: Abraham Lincoln survives assassination (the preacher has to use Lincoln for his hero because there are no American religious heroes the equivalent of Elijah) and goes to Russia, where Lenin nurses him back to health. Lincoln then emancipates the Russian peasants and becomes their hero instead of ours. (This scenario still won't arouse our emotions as much as Jesus' story inflamed his neighbors, but it's a start.)

The second story Jesus told was even worse. He reminded his hearers of the miraculous healing of Naaman, a Syrian army captain who had leprosy, by Elijah's successor, Elisha. This healing occurred at a time when there were "many lepers in Israel . . . and none of them was cleansed except Naaman the Syrian" (Luke 4:27). To catch some sense of the Galileans' ire, you only have to look at any recent newspaper to see how the Israelis and Syrians feel about one another. (Don't forget that Galilee is on the Syrian border.) Imagine a modern Jewish prophet today standing on the former temple mount in Jerusalem or at the Wailing Wall, telling of a one-eyed Syrian general whose eyesight was miraculously restored by God, while Moshe Dyan in Jerusalem remained blind. Little wonder those good people rose up in blind anger to kill this neighbor's boy, whose head somehow had been turned by traitorous liberal ideas. The idea! they cried. God's exclusive grace to Israel going to foreigners, and Israel's worst enemies at that!

Jesus experienced opposition for the same reason throughout his short ministry. He preached of a kingdom of God, or a reign of God, in which outsiders, even sinners, were included in God's grace without the approval of the temple hierarchy. At Nazareth he probably could have gotten away with criticism of the world of religious intrigue at Jerusalem (like criticizing Washington in Texas). But his point would not have been understood. In Galilee, however, where land, the third pillar of Judaism along with the Law and the Temple, was everything, Jesus preached of the blessings of God coming onto foreign soil. His sermon spoke of the unconditional grace of God breaking through Israel's walls of nationalistic self-interest. But if God's grace was equally available to outsiders—even to the enemy—where was God's special favor to Israel? Such teaching must have been terrifying, as well as shocking, to Jesus' neighbors.

During the Vietnam War, a college student in the South was asked to speak about his deepest convictions to his home church during Christmas holidays. The student, who deeply opposed the war as immoral, said that he didn't think the church wanted to hear his deepest convictions. But his pastor insisted, so he spoke. The student was right. His neighbors were shocked and upset at his words, and afterward he was largely shunned by the very people that had taught him his ideals as a child.

The approval of the Nazareth congregation turned to rage when Jesus contradicted their nationalism, confused as religion. He managed to escape from their murderous intent. But we are never told that he returned to his hometown. Like Elijah, who had to find nurture in a foreign land, Jesus had to find a following and a family elsewhere.

Later the experience would be repeated at the feast of Simon, the Pharisee. Simon refused the simplest courtesies to Jesus while a poor woman wept tears on his feet and wiped his feet with her hair. The Pharisee angrily denounced Jesus as no prophet, else he would have known the woman was "a sinner." Jesus told Simon that he had not performed even minimal courtesies, but this woman had not stopped bathing his feet with her tears since he came in. For her great love, Jesus said, her sins, "which were many," were forgiven. Again, the dinner guests were shocked. Jesus had extended the grace of God to those who were yet unworthy, apart from any ritual of priest or temple.

Remember, Jesus was not doing those "new" things because he despised Judaism, or because he intended to renounce Judaism and establish a new religion. He was practicing the faith of Abraham,

Isaac, and Jacob as he believed God intended from the beginning. He was interpreting what he regarded as the lesser things of the Law—ritual, Sabbath rules, purity issues—by what he regarded as the greater things of the Law—love, mercy, and grace.

Within the Old Testament itself a great struggle is evident. In books such as Ezra, Nehemiah, and First and Second Chronicles, a more restrictive view of Judaism and God's favor appears. Books such as Ruth and Jonah present a more inclusive attitude toward outsiders. Furthermore, the larger Old Testament shows another powerful tension: one between priestly and prophetic emphases. The priestly sections (the documents in the Pentateuch identified by scholars as P) emphasize Israel's cultic duty to God. These are typically reflected in temple observances and offerings. This priestly product magnifies those things that required the authority of the priests. The word *chesed*, referring to the lovingkindness of God, does not appear in the priestly document. Nor does the word for repentance. In other words, if somebody wanted to get right with God, priests were indispensable.

The prophets, on the other hand, saw the hypocrisy of much of the external cultic observances of Israel. They emphasized inner repentance—"rend your heart and not your clothing" (Joel 2:13)—with justice toward the weak and the poor, and the grace of God as the only hope for a wayward people. For the "sins of the high hand" (Num 15:30-31), willful sin against God, there would be no sacrifice or offering. What hope was there for such sinners? Only this: "A broken and contrite heart, O God, you will not despise" (Ps 51:17).

The activity of Jesus plainly continued this prophetic tradition. In fact, he radically extended its inclusive emphasis to the most excluded of society: lepers, tax collectors (traitors), and women of all sorts, including prostitutes. For this reason, "the large crowd was listening to him with delight" (Mark 12:37).

Nonetheless, this message also makes it plain why he was hated by officialdom and eventually killed. Such preaching of grace destabilized the establishment and empowered the masses. Land, law, and temple were held under the authority of the aristocracy and their appointees. These three equaled social control. Jesus disputed the religious establishment's understanding of the Law, demonstrated dramatically against the temple, and insisted that the grace of God extended beyond the borders of the land. Without social control, the aristocracy could not guarantee tranquility to their Roman masters for whom rebellion was the unforgivable sin. The man was plainly dangerous to those in control; he had to die. Rome had the power to do that; the aristocracy had the motive to do it.

Jesus was not a "Christian" killed by "the Jews." The separation of the Jews who followed Jesus as Messiah from the synagogues lay years in the future. Jesus was a Jew who believed in the prophetic tradition. Like Amos, he was a common man who believed that Yahweh despised the aristocratic abuse of the poor. He was killed because of his threat to the aristocratic establishment and the Romans who put them in power.

Israel still considered itself a theocracy, a nation governed by God. Therefore its only governing body, the Sanhedrin, was controlled by the high priest and other aristocratic leaders. The Jewish aristocracy repudiated Jesus for fear of the Romans; the Romans killed him for fear of a peasant uprising. (The peasant revolt only thirty years later showed they definitely had something to fear from such a charismatic peasant figure.) But his unwavering commitment to radical, inclusive grace doomed him from the beginning.

Is Grace Obsolete?

In our modern, secular world of multinational corporations and power politics, such a religious notion as grace may seem quaint at best and ludicrous at worst. That grace, inclusive or not, could ever be a player in major world drama seems unlikely or ridiculous. That differences over a theological question could affect history is virtually inconceivable to our secular world. Who cares about grace on that stage? Let synagogue or temple or church or seminary lose sleep over such issues. But outside the realm of the religious, the question of "grace" today is largely irrelevant.

On the other hand, Robert Coles, noted Harvard sociologist and psychiatrist, regards an understanding of grace in the biblical sense essential for moral transformation of the individual and society:

> I remember a conversation with Erik Erikson back in the late 1960s. He was himself remembering a conversation with some psychoanalytic colleagues. The subject was Gandhi, his method of taking on the British, his way of living a life. Erikson had spent years trying to understand the Mahatma (the result was Gandhi's Truth), and in so doing had come to realize how difficult it is to

"explain" psychologically the astonishing moral vitality of such a person.

As he tried to do just that, tell a few psychoanalysts what qualities of mind made for a particular leader, he found himself using the word "grace" again and again. Eventually he was challenged. What did he mean by that word "grace"? How would he define it? What explains its appearance in one or another person? "I told them," Erikson told me, "that I didn't know how to answer their questions—that if you are in the presence of grace, you sure know it, and you sure feel grateful."

His listeners, he knew, were not satisfied. Nor is it fair to accuse that handful of psychiatric specialists of being especially obtuse, wrongheaded, or narrowly reductionist. . . . Words such as "grace" are a relic (aren't they?) of another (pre-scientific) age, when men and women didn't understand the way the mind works, the way society comes to bear on the individual.[2]

Apparently, however, grace is not quite the relic our modern power-brokers think. Bill Moyers devoted an hour's television documentary on public broadcasting to the song, "Amazing Grace." The program wasn't about music, though music was included. Nor was it merely a story of religious beliefs about the doctrine of grace. The theme of the program really concerned the power of an idea, the idea of unconditional grace. People from all races and every station of life told of the transforming power of a loving acceptance that is not conditioned on propriety of any sort, religious or secular. It was not difficult to see the empowering nature of such a belief to common people. Nor was it difficult to imagine the threat of exploited people who had just discovered their self-worth to entrenched social establishments anywhere.

Make no mistake: grace is the power of the message of Jesus. Wherever it has been believed and put into practice, whether in Rome or in South Africa, grace has empowered its practitioners. It also has put them in danger. In religious disputes, such as the roles of clergy and laity in the church or the place of women, it has disrupted established hierarchical systems. In such secular issues as the integration of races in the South or the place of women in society, it has destabilized the aristocratic assumptions of the establishment. Where grace has triumphed, it has liberated minorities and brought life to the neediest

Grace

in society. Wherever the grace of Jesus has come to live, hate cannot find lodging.

The most moving story of grace I have ever heard was told by Frederick G. Sampson, pastor of Mount Lebanon Baptist Church in Louisville, Kentucky. When he was a child, his grandmother told him of the lynching of her son. He was accused of raping a white girl, and a mob seized him and lynched him before the authorities learned he was really innocent. When his grandmother heard of his murder, she went to the jail and claimed his body. She took her dead child home and washed his body. Then she dressed him in his Sunday clothes, and his family buried him in secret. Sampson's grandmother returned home, changed her clothes into a maid's uniform, and walked up to the big house on the hill where she worked for a white family. She went into the two children's bedroom, kissed them and woke them as usual, then prepared their breakfast and sent them off to school.

At that point in his grandmother's story, Sampson interrupted her. "But Granny! Why didn't you kill them white kids the way they killed your boy!" She took him in her arms and looked him the eye. "Sonny boy, when you got Jesus in your heart, you just can't hate anybody."

That kind of grace is costly. Even when it is admired as an ideal, it is usually put off as unworkable. That was the history of the Year of Jubilee. The famous Rabbi Hillel (shortly before the time of Jesus) instituted the *prozbul,* a decree of exemption, that allowed debts to continue through the Sabbatical Year.[3] Some of the stricter groups in Israel today still seek a *prozbul* to avoid the requirements of such a year. Paradise is a great idea—but not now. Putting off paradise has become an art for all of us, Christians and Jews alike. Unlimited forgiveness and inclusiveness are fine in theory, but most of us prefer paradise postponed. It costs too much.

Does the Church Believe in Grace?

What about the church? Does the church believe in grace? Of course it does. What does the church believe more than "God's unmerited favor"? Of course, Paul and James got off to an early start on debates over grace and works, which the Roman Catholic church and the Protestant churches managed to keep going a couple of millennia or so. As usual, these doctrinal debates occupied more of the churches' time than the practice of the doctrine in question. As one theologian put it, our orthodoxy has long since outstripped our orthopraxy. These days, however, theologians generally agree that grace and works are complementary.

We believe in grace, but we exercise grace selectively. Culture tends to call the shots for us. Outsiders are alright if they don't threaten our territory. They are welcome if they are compliant with our customs or our way of doing church—our liturgy or lack of it, our fondness for Bach or string quartets instead of the Stamps Brothers and gospel quartets—especially if they understand that our economic interests and various prejudices are clearly endorsed by the Bible.

A visitor to a British Sunday School for street urchins, taught by an aristocratic *grande dame,* was reportedly startled to hear her young disciples chirping in unison the prayer she had taught them: "O God, confirm the wealthy in their riches and restrain the vicious poor!"

The opposite picture of grace is shown in the example of Dick Sheppard and Saint Martin's Church in London. In 1914 Sheppard became vicar of Saint Martin-in-the-Fields and resolved to follow his vision for it:

> I stood on the west steps and saw what this church would be to the life of the people. There passed me, into its warm inside, hundreds and hundreds of all sorts of people, going up to the temple of their Lord, with all their difficulties, trials, and sorrows. I saw it full of people dropping in at all hours of the day and night. It was never dark, it was lighted all night and all day, and often tired bits of humanity swept in. And I said to them as they passed, "Where are you going?" And they said only one thing. "This is our home. This is where we are going to learn of the love of Jesus Christ. This is the altar of our Lord, where all our peace lies. This is St. Martin's." It was all reverent and full of love, and they never pushed me behind a pillar because I was poor.[4]

Many changes took place at St. Martin's after Dick Sheppard went to the church. Reserved pews were abolished. Parts of the church were opened to the homeless, and food was provided. Everyone, rich or poor, was invited and included. Saint Martin's became a different kind of place. Sheppard recorded:

> St. Martin's Church became the church of the soldiers and the down-and-outs; the church of the classes and masses; the church of fellowship and of privacy; the church for the cheerful and the

church for the desperate; the church for the healthy and the sick; of the young and the old. It was the church in which the congregation was no more shocked at hearing the minister pray for the streetwalkers than pray for schoolteachers, for crooks than for the clergy, for blackguards than for bishops; no more shocked than when the vicar laughed and told a funny story in the pulpit. It became a refuge for the unhappy and the home of the homeless. In short, it was a Christian church.[5]

Our grace in the Christian church, unfortunately, has not amounted generally to much more than the narrow inclusiveness of any common-interest society. Church membership is often more like a religious affinity card than the radical union of socially and politically unlikes that Jesus gathered about him, those diverse souls he called his *ecclesia,* his church.

But where the true church has triumphed over special interests an amazing, transforming power is released into society. Paradise is postponed no more. The "year of jubilee" finally begins. Old debts really are cancelled: from father against son, clan against clan, race against race. Land is shared: opportunities are equal across lines of gender or race, opportunities to vote or get an education or sit in the front of society's bus. And the temple is thrown open to the imperfect, the deformed of society; even eunuchs and Gentiles may enter (Isa 56:3-7; Acts 8:38). Gentiles may become priests, and daughters as well as sons may preach (Joel 2:28), for "my house shall be called a house of prayer for all the nations" (Isa 56:7; Mark 11:17).

The Oasis of Life

In the first century, Jesus told his neighbors at Nazareth that paradise had been impossible long enough. Now at the end of the twentieth century, are we yet ready to begin "the acceptable day of the Lord," the grace that stands as an oasis of life in this arid world of privilege and poverty?

In the early days of this country, Ogalala, Nebraska, was once described as the dry, treeless, heartless heart of America. In those first days of westward migration, many would-be settlers lost their farms and lives there due to lack of water. On an abandoned sod hut someone discovered a sign, left there by a westbound traveler. The sign read: "This would be fine country if it just had water." A bitter old sod-buster had written on the sign in reply, "Yeah, and so would hell!"

Neither sign writer knew that just beneath the dusty wagon tracks lay the Ogalala aquifer, one of the largest underground rivers on this planet. Its resources are great enough to bury all fifty states a foot-and-a-half deep in water. This High Plains aquifer, the largest underground water system in the United States, is sometimes called the "Sixth Great Lake." It is an amazing underground sea, holding as much water as Lake Huron plus one-fifth of Lake Ontario. But until its life-giving contents are brought to the surface, the parched sod-buster goes without water, and the scorched plains still are hell on earth.

The reservoir of God's grace is limitless and abundant. The life of Jesus revealed its availability to each of us. Through God's gift it resides in us, just beneath the surface. God has seen to that. Nevertheless, as long as it lies submerged, paradise is postponed and the climate on earth too closely resembles a medieval hell. But when we tap that source and share it with others, the deserts of human life bloom like the rose, and new life springs up everywhere.

Robert Coles uses great literature to teach great truths to his "young, would-be physicians" at Harvard Medical School. They find particularly compelling two Tolstoy stories that portray two men finding life for the first time as they die. The first story, "The Death of Ivan Ilych" tells of a cold, inconsiderate lawyer who finds humanity and reconciliation with his family through a servant who cares for him as he is dying.

The second story, "Master and Man," written some ten years later, similarly recounts the story of a businessman obsessed with greed, whose last hours are spent in a terrifying blizzard. He has insisted, insanely, that his servant press on through the storm. Now he and the servant and their horse are trapped. The servant quietly awaits death while his master rages; the horse stoically accepts his fate. At last, in this frozen hell, the master finds a spark of human warmth within himself. His last act is to place his body over that of his simple servant; and dying, he finds life. Coles wrote:

> These two Tolstoy stories tell us of life's redemptive possibilities; remind us that those who by secular standards have a lot can be in terrible spiritual jeopardy, and indeed, can be spared hell only through the mediation of a humble one, even as Jesus himself lived

a humble life; and finally, insist that the time we have here is never over until the very end, no matter the various (psychological and sociological) determinisms, the stages and phases and complexes of various theorists who would have us marching like automatons through life. The book of our lives is open—even until the last breath. With these haunting tales Tolstoy admonishes us—but also invites us—to risk the saving grace of brotherly love, an opportunity for which may fall upon us out of nowhere, it seems, and enliven us in preparation for that last and most important journey to meet our Maker.[6]

We speak often of our "cold, cruel world." Jesus offers the warmth of God's grace to all who are trapped in the lifeless, inhuman coldness of loneliness, fear, and indifference. We don't have to buy this garment of grace. It is the robe that the waiting Father gives to all prodigals who "come to themselves" and turn toward home.

Harry Emerson Fosdick once said,

> On the day I left for college, I gave my house key to my father; but my father returned it, saying, "My boy, you keep the key and let it be a symbol as long as you live that you can come home anytime from anywhere and come in without knocking."

That was the message of Jesus, the message of grace: a lost key to life and the key that unlocks our understanding of the other keys Jesus shared with ordinary people like us.

Notes

[1] Walter Bruggemann, *Finally Comes the Poet* (Minneapolis: Fortress, 1989) 146.

[2] Robert Coles, *Harvard Diary: Reflections on the Sacred and the Secular* (New York: Crossroad, 1988) 102-103.

[3] Lawrence H. Schiffman, "Sabbatical Year," *Harper's Bible Dictionary*, ed. Paul J. Achtemeier (San Francisco: Harper, 1985): 889.

[4] Hazel Tourtel, *St. Martin-in-the-Fields: A Short History* (a booklet prepared by the parish historian of St. Martin-in-the-Fields) 25.

[5] Richard Ellis Roberts, *H. R. L. Sheppard: Life and Letters* (London: John Murray, 1942) 93.

[6] Coles, 197.

Chapter 3

LAW

From Psalmist's Delight to Puritan's Despair

We can understand grace as a key or meaning to life. But law? Can law open doors? Doesn't law in fact slam doors? Keys say access; law says refusal. Grace and mercy say yes; law says no. Sympathy understands; law believes they had it coming. If law is a key to life, it must be one that only locks doors, not opens them.

Yet the psalmist and the writers of Proverbs somehow had a different view: "O how I love your law" (Ps 119:97). "Happy are those who keep the law" (Prov 29:18). "Their delight is in the law of the Lord, and on his law they meditate day and night" (Ps 1:2). These days the words "happiness" and "delight" are not usually associated with law. What is the difference in this ancient Hebrew understanding of God's law and ours? Why did the Hebrews love the law that so intimidates us? Why did they see the law as a happy evidence of God, while to us it seems little more than a frowning caricature of a cosmic bully?

Law as Delight

To begin with, the translation of the Hebrew word *torah* as "law" is somewhat misleading. Except for late biblical tradition when Law meant the Pentateuch, the word always had a broader meaning. Dietrich Bonhoeffer wrote:

> Torah, the law, originally meant that which was determined by casting lots . . . Torah is God's cast of the lots over humanity. It goes beyond all human thought and expectation. "The lot is fallen unto me in a fair ground; yea, I have a goodly heritage" (Ps 16:7). God's judgment is grace and life for human beings; it is life before God and with God through the forgiveness of sins. . . . Not an "it," an idea, but a "thou" meets us in the commandments. A further sign of this is found in the Hebrew word for "commandments" in this verse (Ps 119:4). It is a word which cannot be translated by a single word of ours. It derives from the verb for seeking, visiting, paying

attention to. Hence, the commandments are what God looks at, pays attention to, and the means by which he seeks and visits the human being. The commandments then reflect God's way towards the human being.[1]

In other words, the *torah* of God is the entire will of God for humankind. *Torah* is not simply a collection of rules, a dry, impersonal code to be posted on the employee's bulletin board of life. *Torah* is the encounter of God with humanity through events as well as through decrees, narrative, poetry, and wisdom literature. In Psalms 1:2 the delight of the psalmist is not in the particularities of Hebrew law, but in the gift of divine revelation itself.

Torah can also mean simply the "teaching" or "instruction" of the Lord. *Torah* is something God has taught to humankind. The psalmist delighted in what God had said, as opposed to the babble of voices from the world. Persons who walk in the light of this revelation are happy and secure. They are like trees planted by streams of water. Those who do not walk in this truth are blown around like the weightless chaff from the wheat (Ps 1:3-4). When Moses made his farewell speech, which occupies the whole book of Deuteronomy, he gave Israel an additional body of laws (chaps. 12-26) that he called "this *torah*." Likewise, when prophets such as Isaiah used *torah*, it referred to the Word of God that came to them as prophecy. In every case, however, whether in the Pentateuch or the psalms or the prophets, the emphasis is on the divine origin of the commands.

Following their bitter experience in exile, *torah* took on new meaning to Israel. Beginning with Ezra, the Law, now understood as the Pentateuch, became the whole basis of the life of Israel.[2] The reason was simple. Israel believed that its captivity in Babylonia resulted from disobedience to the Law. It therefore resolved not to make the same mistake twice. For the individual, obedience to the Law was necessary to retain membership in the community of faith. The same was true for the nation. If the nation disobeyed, it would be cast away from God's favor. With the development of the synagogue, which gradually emerged as the center of teaching of the Law, further emphasis was placed on the Law in the daily life of Israel.

One's ancestry also became increasingly important. After all, didn't those foreign gods brought in by foreign wives lead Israel astray? (Eve is neatly blamed again for this second Fall; see Ezra 9–10, when

Gentile wives and their children were packed up and sent away.) Jews were to marry true Jews only (Deut 7:1-6). Israel clearly had been a mixed people at its beginning, made up of many tribes and nations, and only slowly bound together by a worship of Yahweh. Nevertheless, after the Babylonian captivity, only ethnic purity was considered a reliable safeguard against religious corruption.

No doubt the scrupulous work of Ezra was necessary to hold distinct the identity of this tiny, weak nation and its peculiar religion of one God. Without it, the Jews probably would have been assimilated into their surrounding Semitic neighbors. But such external safeguards breed internal troubles. The prophets had already complained about external observances without internal faith. Isaiah recorded these words of the Lord:

> What to me is the multitude of your sacrifices? . . . I have had enough of burnt offerings of rams and the fat of fed beasts; I do not delight in the blood of bulls, or of lambs, or of goats. When you come to appear before me, who asked this from your hand? Trample my courts no more; bringing offerings is futile; incense is an abomination to me.
>
> New moon and sabbath and calling of convocation—I cannot endure solemn assemblies with iniquity. Your new moons and your appointed festivals my soul hates; they have become a burden to me, I am weary of bearing them. When you stretch out your hands, I will hide my eyes from you; even though you make many prayers, I will not listen; your hands are full of blood.
>
> Wash yourselves; make yourselves clean; remove the evil of your doings from before my eyes; cease to do evil, learn to do good; seek justice, rescue the oppressed, defend the orphan, plead for the widow. (1:11-17)

Such demands plainly could not be met by mere external conformity to marriage laws or ritual sacrifices. Bonhoeffer spoke of the inner requirements of God's decrees:

> The decrees are the warning signs which God has set up on the way of his people, so that they do not go astray. The Hebrew word used here is often translated "testimonies" [*edah*]. It first came into frequent use in the Babylonian captivity. There the people realized in the time of punishment and expiation that the commandments had been given as warnings and reminders of God, the Lord (Neh 9:34).

God gives such testimonies to his people on their way so that in the time of trial they might know that in the end he will do them good (Deut 8:16). Since God is the Lord of whom his decrees should daily remind us and to whom they should testify, no external observance of them can suffice. Not only lips and hands but the whole, undivided heart must be involved; it must be eternally seeking the One of whom the testimonies speak.[3]

But this larger concept of law was never favored by the Aaronic priesthood. The so-called P document in the Pentateuch reflected their views. This priestly source eliminated the earlier stories of the Pentateuch in which God communicated through angels, dreams, or even animals. All criticism of Aaron, as in his making of the golden calf, was also eliminated. The point of these omissions was to emphasize that access to God was only possible through priestly channels, principally through offerings and sacrifices. This exclusive emphasis on cultic practices as the sole means of access to God found favor in the strict interpretations of Ezra following the disaster of the Babylonian captivity.

Most important for our purposes, in this entire document the words mercy/merciful (*rhm*), grace/gracious (*hnn*), repent/repentance (*swb*), or lovingkindness (*hsd*)—elsewhere used as a primary attribute of God toward humankind—do not occur even once. In their place, P created a hierarchy of priests, with the Levite occupying a lower course of service. Only those Levites from Aaronic descent remained as priests.

The overall picture is clear. Following their captivity in Babylonia, the Israelites returned shaken, confused, and looking for answers. The priesthood gained new power as it demanded stricter conformity to ritual sacrifice as the only means of pleasing God. In spite of prophetic words to the contrary, external observances remained dominant and institutionalized as Israel's test of fidelity to God. The Aaronic priests were satisfied. Their livelihood was secured, and they remained the principal interpreters of both Law and God.

By the time of the New Testament era, the Law had been elevated to a status almost coexistent with God. Some rabbis taught that when God wanted to beging creating the earth, God consulted the Torah. The priesthood and the temple were elevated in importance as well. But so were the Pharisees, the "separated ones," a lay group dedicated to upholding the Law. No doubt the majority of Pharisees and other religious leaders in Israel were intent only on inculcating true piety and devotion to the Lord. But a welter of conflicting oral interpretations had grown up about the Law, and many of the common people (the "people of the land") despaired of understanding it. They did not, probably could not, keep the Pharisaic rules of purity, food, and tithing. No doubt some felt the sentiments expressed in the words of Jesus found in Matthew 23:23-26:

> Woe to you, scribes and Pharisees, hypocrites! For you tithe mint, dill, and cummin, and have neglected the weightier matters of the law: justice and mercy and faith. It is these you ought to have practiced without neglecting the others. You blind guides! You strain out a gnat but swallow a camel!
> Woe to you, scribes and Pharisees, hypocrites! For you clean the outside of the cup and of the plate, but inside they are full of greed and self-indulgences. You blind Pharisee! First clean the inside of the cup, so that the outside also may become clean.

Both the Babylonian and Palestinian Talmud also list various classes of hypocritical Pharisees, though the accuracy of these sources for a description of first-century Pharisees has been questioned. But even when due allowances are made for the possibility of such statements as accommodation to early Christian influences, the natural rivalries and hostilities of the diverse and competing Jewish groups with one another must be kept in mind. Remember also that in the time of Jesus the dominant religious issue was not Christian versus Jew, or vice-versa, but strict interpretation of the Torah versus liberal interpretation. Politically, the conflict focused on ruling aristocratic groups versus the powerless but dangerous peasants.

If the priests and scribes and Pharisees were hostile toward the new Jesus movement, and if he answered back sharply, we must remember that these were nonetheless Jews contending with one another over the true understanding of *torah*. For Jesus, that meant inclusiveness, widening the criteria for acceptability before God, even wider than the most liberal parties of his time. That alone would have been sufficient cause for heated opposition to his movement by the competing parties within first century Judaism.

The rabbis spoke often of the "yoke of the Law." Jesus described his way by the phrase, "My yoke is easy" (Matt 11:30). Paul warned Christians in his time against submitting "again to a yoke of slavery" (Gal 5:1). Both of these expressions refer to the opinion current among some people that the Law once regarded as a gift and a delight had become a legalistic burden. Jesus encouraged his followers to become yoked with him and learn of him; his yoke was "kind," not heavy or oppressive. He was regarded personally as "gentle and humble in heart" (Matt 11:29); in contrast to the arrogant religious authorities who boasted of their righteousness (23:4). To the law-burdened he offered rest, for his burden was light (11:30).

Jesus was not offering careless, libertarian living, but relief from meaningless external details and a renewed emphasis on the "weightier matters of the law, justice and mercy and faith" (Matt 23:23). In his Sabbath controversies, Jesus reminded the rigorous sabbatarians of the words of God from Hosea, "I desire steadfast love and not sacrifice" (6:6). Paul's letter to the Galatians seems also to be warning those Christians against returning to a legalistic life.

How, then, did we get where the church is today? Jesus plainly favored grace and mercy over judgmental attitudes, and Paul argued consistently against the "slavery" of legalism. How is it that the average U.S. citizen today regards Christianity as a blue-nosed, nay-saying religion of negativism? Our generation holds much the same opinion as Swinburne who wrote these words a century ago: "O, pale Galilean, the world has grown gray from at thy breath" ("Hymn to Proserphine"). But in the first century, Jesus breathed color in the cheeks of a world grown pale with exhaustion from ritualistic systems and nearly bled white by the self-serving autocrats of religion. How is it that in our century the yoke of Christ is regarded as irritating and his burden as heavy?

As Paul's correspondence reveals, it wasn't long before many who joined the new Way simply didn't get it. They brought into the new gathering of Jesus, the "church" of Jesus, their old understanding of religion. Salvation demands hard duties; religious societies provide secret knowledge. If the medicine is to work, it must taste bad. This is the "common sense" understanding of human religion. The Mayans in Central America later were typical of this view. They built all of their civic buildings with normal entrance steps. But the steps to their temple-pyramids were narrow and steep. Their symbolism was clear. The way to God is difficult; only those who watch their step can ascend. Love of neighbor and love of God as the sum of the law? Salvation as the gift of God? Too easy. Common sense tells us that we must pay for sins with duties, rituals, and offerings. As the church grew, it slowly reverted to the legalistic superstitions of "common sense" religion.

So the early church, even before the death of Paul—and certainly afterward, as manifested in the Pastoral Epistles and later Christian writings—quickly reversed the saying of Jesus. Instead of practicing the weightier matters of the law, the early Christians set up a new religious legalism based on whatever "rules" and details they could glean from the teachings of Jesus and Paul, but particularly Paul, whose complex theology better suited the purpose. "Love of God and neighbor" was too general. What exactly does love of God entail? Love of neighbor? Soon the church was spelling out in detail the "rules" for the worthy, but too vague principles of Jesus.

Of course, the rules that emerged came straight from the customs of each generation. Whatever "good men"—and it was men—already knew to be true and "moral," by their common sense and local practice, was established as gospel truth. Sometimes far-fetched interpretations of obscure scripture verses had to be employed to proof-text these rules. But they knew such a text had to be there somewhere in the Bible; after all, they knew what they believed was true anyhow.

For example, Galileo was banned from using his telescope in Florence by the text, "Men of Galilee, why do you stand looking up toward heaven?" (Acts 1:11). In many other cases as well, sayings of Jesus or Paul were interpreted "literally," that is, as anyone with common sense (in the sixteenth century or whenever) would understand them. No matter that originally the context of the saying was entirely different. The verse, "Anyone unwilling to work should not eat" (2 Thess 3:10), was said originally against those who quit working in anticipation of the second coming of Christ. It had nothing to do with welfare for the poor.

If there simply was no parallel in the Bible, no matter how hard the scrupulous looked, the legalists' prohibitions against "known evil" —such as dancing Baptists, tippling Methodists, Sabbath-enjoying Presbyterians—were justified by appealing to a protective hedge of their own oral traditions. These rules were as strict as any ever laid down by the opponents of Jesus. The Puritans, and their many descendants, made a science out of this legalistic rule-stretching.

Nothing before or since has had such widespread effect on the American understanding of law in religion as the early Puritan movement in the New England colonies. Particularly in the Massachussets Bay Colony, the Puritans so stood the gospel of Jesus on its head that it has never quite regained its balance. Their extreme legalism left behind a dual legacy in this country. First, the Christian religion in America, perhaps more than anywhere else, continues to struggle internally against a literalistic and judgmental understanding of the Bible. Second, those outside Christian circles, including millions in America who have left the church, despise the moralistic tone they understand to be the dominant voice of the Christian message. What did the Puritans bring to our understanding of the place of law in the Christian faith? And why?

Legalism and Religion in American

To their credit, initially the Puritans had a good idea. J. I. Packer, a British Puritan scholar, said that the Puritans never sought to create a morbid and introspective piety. Rather, they "ripped up conscience in the pulpit and urged self-trial in the closet only to drive sinners to Christ and to teach them to live by faith in him."[4] The Puritans believed in making specific applications of the gospel to human lives, a point at which they felt the church had greatly failed. Packer said that they

> did not wish men's consciences to be bound by their own teaching, as such, but to the Word of God only, and to Puritan teaching only so far as it was demonstrably in accord with the Word of God.[5]

Nevertheless, some reasons for their future troubles, and ours, can be seen in Packer's two rulings axioms of Puritan life:

> No known truth must be compromised or denied in practice, and no avoidable sin must be committed, no matter how great the good to which such compromise and sin may lead.[6]

These are logical principles, but it isn't hard to see how the effecting of them might easily lead to harshness and legalism. Especially when Packer says that the name Puritan is not as proper a name for the group as "Precisians," the early name applied to them, and that "if there were such a thing as a Puritan crest," its motto would be, "I serve a precise God."[7]

To be fair to the Puritan preachers, there was breadth to their moral preaching. The first New England sermon that found its way into print was concerned with an economic problem and was devoted to saving the colony from disaster.[8] Other sermons were frequently devoted to the ethics of trade, for example, John Cotton's notable sermon on that subject in 1639 and the frequent sermons of Hugh Peter in Boston and Salem. Meanwhile, William Hooke and Samuel Nowell spoke on war and politics, though on opposite sides. Though strongly moral in their teaching and preaching, the Puritans weren't as prudish as they have been pictured. One of John Cotton's marriage sermons, preached in 1694, would stun the average bride of the 1990s.

The Puritans also were not above a bit of situation ethics when the occasion demanded. Listen to these divorce regulations by the Cambridge ministers:

> Article VII. In case of a *malicious desertion* by a married person, who is . . . invited to return, a divorce may be granted by lawful authority unto the forsaken. For the word of God is plain, "that a Christian is not bound in such cases" by the marriage unto one which has thus wilfully violated the covenant; and tho' our Saviour forbids "a man's putting away his wife, except it be for fornication," yet he forbids not rulers to rescue an innocent person from the enthralling disadvantages of another that shall sinfully go away.[9]
>
> Article IX. A divorce being legally pursued and obtained, the innocent person that is released may proceed unto a "second marriage in the Lord." Otherwise the state of believers under the New Testament would in some of these cases be worse than what the God of heaven directed for his people under the Old."[10]

But this in itself suggests one of the principal errors of the Puritans in the 1600s and of Puritans in subsequent centuries. They believed that every activity of life, to the smallest detail, could find a law in the Bible. The search for those laws pressed them to the most ridiculous extremes. Even when they had papered the walls of their moral world with every page from both the Old and New Testaments, there was still a lot of bare wall showing. So they used a combination of allegory, imagination, and the wildest interpretation imaginable to cover the gaps. All of this far-fetched interpretation, of course, was interpreted strictly as "abiding by the Word of God."

The Puritan preachers were trapped also by another crushing force. They were obligated to become jurists for the New England colony. The Puritans sought to establish a way of life based upon biblical authority. With their literal view of the Bible and their refusal to admit the possibility of variations of interpretation, they set about building an inflexible legal system upon their current interpretations of the Bible. Who would administer such a system of biblical law? The Puritan preachers, of course.

Soon they were lost in a nightmare of tangled interpretations. According to Kai T. Erickson,

> Does the law against adultery apply when an English settler is found lying with an Indian women? Every day the courts seemed to discover some frightful new sin for which there was no precedent in biblical history.[11]

During the first years of the colony, the preachers had to settle most of these questions of law. When they failed to find a specific biblical rule for the case—which happened often—they were forced to establish one based upon community mores. The net result was the establishment of a set of unbending oral laws based on nothing more than the whims of society at the moment. By attempting to cover everything, the Puritans failed at precisely the thing they had dreaded. They had abandoned the Word of God for the "whims of man."

Then the Puritans began to enforce these "eternal laws," which were actually based on nothing more than the recent customs of their fathers, with a vengeance. The original energy of the group that had been expended on non-conformity now became utilized for demanding conformity to the group. The dissenting society was faced with the troubling issue of what to do with their own dissenters. The answer? Simple: make them conform. Those who once had been willing to suffer punishment, even death, for the right to interpret the Word of God freely began to punish any among them who did that very thing. Without realizing it, the Puritans became as oppressive a society as the one they had fled.

Every Puritan became an informer on his neighbors. In one sermon Thomas Bray urged:

> Why, if you find yourselves possessed of a noble and heroic spirit, if you feel in your breast a generous ardor, if you thirst for glory, and affect the post of honor, turn informers. These are they who offer and present themselves for the grand attack; these bravely scale the walls of sin; these carry off the devil's vassals captives after them to

the tribunal of the Christian magistrates, to receive their sentence and suffer . . . punishment.[12]

Soon there were informers aplenty. Everyone knew how many dresses Goodwife Smythe had in her closet and what her temper was like if the cow kicked over the pail. The pulpit scolded; Goodwife Smythe suffered punishment.

Since their laws were based on the customs of the fathers, the children rebelled. The parents sulked. They had given birth, they were convinced, to an evil generation. Soon their pessimism became official dogma. The Puritans firmly believed that the best days had been, and that each generation would be worse than the first. Because they expected bad boys, they got them. In their rebellion the children were forced to reject not only the customs of the fathers, but also the Word of God, since the two were identified by the church as one and the same. Since moralistic snooping was part of their ethic, quite naturally the children were quick to spot hypocrisy. One of the Puritans' own preachers said it most painfully: "New England hath many godly men in it, but few honest."[13]

As a result of their legalistic preaching, the Puritans lost the very thing they came to America to save: the faith of their children. Even worse, they lost the faith of the children's children, for "the sins of the fathers shall be visited upon the children to the third and fourth generations." The verb "to preach" has never been the same since the legalism of the New England Puritans.

The Law That Opens Doors

Has the mote-finding and log-ignoring of the Puritan eye caused Americans to regard God's law as a curse rather than a blessing? How then can law be called a key to life? Let me suggest several principles that can guide us back to the true sense of law as delight, an essential key to life in our desperate, addled world.

(1) *Our modern notion of autonomy is a fantasy.* We are not free, and we are not free of law. Our opinions are never "our own." We are social creatures, bound up with one another in a society of incalculable influence. What we eat, what we wear, how we vote, the very language and idioms we speak come from below rather than from above—in Jesus' words to the confused Nicodemus—from our

culture. The law of Christ, on the other hand, breaks the mold of me, my, mine: my country, my clan, my kin, right or wrong; my possessions, my skin color, my sectionalism. The exclusiveness of the laws we live by, unwritten as well as written, contrast ultimately with the inclusiveness of God's laws. To live by God's laws is to know freedom. To live by our laws is to know provincial slavery in but another state of human selfishness, alienation, and rage. As Walter Bruggeman wrote,

> We imagined that we were the children of modernity: liberated, autonomous, on our own. We thought the speech of this other One [God] had been banished and with good riddance. But the ideology of autonomy is not sufficient. It leads eventually to alienation, isolation, and rage. In our autonomous silence, we deny our true selves, created as we are, for conversation, communion, trust, and yielding.[14]

The church must declare the fallacy of all notions of freedom apart from the word of God—including its own. The church cannot wield the sword of the Word as if it is its own weapon, to be used as it likes. The church must always stand beneath the very Word it declares. The preacher of the Word must repent at the very words he/she speaks. The world resents true preaching because it challenges its fantasy of autonomy. The conventional church often resents true preaching because it contradicts conventional wisdom, the things everyone knows to be true. (The strange thing is how the church never notices that its neighbors largely think the same as it does, even if they have no notion of the gospel.) Stanley Hauerwas said,

> The very activity of preaching, that is, the proclamation of a story that cannot be known apart from such proclamation, is an affront to the ethos of freedom. As a church, we stand under the word because we know we are told what we otherwise could not know. We stand under the word because we know we need to be told what to do. We stand under the word because we do not believe we have minds worth making up on our own. Such guidance is particularly necessary for people like us who have been corrupted by our tolerance.[15]

(2) *Our confidence in our human system of laws, as a satisfactory safeguard of "our values," apart from the word of God, is a dangerous mistake.* The Enlightenment informed the West of the worth of each

individual and the value of reason over superstition. So far so good. But it overturned the tyranny of superstition and replaced it with the tyranny of rationalism. The medieval church had decided only that which could be established from its tradition was true. The rationalists decided only that which could be established by their rational principles was true.

Both had the same problem, if with quite different results. Both believed their system of laws was absolute and final. Subsequent history has proved them both wrong. The Roman church today is certainly in a different place theologically and ethically than where it was then, and the eighteenth-century rationalists have had their conclusions poked full of philosophical holes.

Nevertheless, in some ways the Enlightenment with all its arrogance may have been closer to the gospel than the church with all its arrogance. The Enlightenment at least pulled the foundation from under the medieval church, which had turned the freedom of the believer in Christ into the domination of ecclesiastical magicians. The subsequent development of the laws of science and the laws of the states represented a positive, even a godly, turn from the superstitions and dictates of an ignorant and venal religious system.

But the modern world now tends to overestimate the power of "rational" secular societies to generate morality and ethic codes. As Eli Sagan said,

> Society will not undertake a moral revolution because it is urged to be rational anymore than a patient in psychotherapy may be cured by being told to cut out the nonsense.[16]

In the development of political states, the Magna Carta and the United States Constitution represented great strides forward. These documents were not, however, infallible. (To those who practice civil religion, of course, this is pure heresy.) In some ways our Bill of Rights moved ahead of its surrounding culture. But when it said, "We hold these truths to be self-evident, that all men are created equal . . . ," it really meant all white men, not black slaves, or even their own wives and daughters. They held those truths "to be self-evident." That was their problem. They were self-evident—to their male, privileged selves in that generation.

Law is forever bound to its own time. Only subsequent interpretation can free it to live in future time. The amendments to the U.S.

Constitution are only a small part of the ongoing process of reinterpreting that law to match the realities of a subsequent world. But the best of laws is not better than the people who administer it. And so far, no law has been written to make better people.

In the play, *A Man for All Seasons,* Thomas More trusted in the security of English law too much, as he would learn. He lectured his son-in-law, William Roper, who would cut down all law to eliminate corruption, on the necessity of giving even the devil the benefit of law:

> Oh? And when the last law was down, and the Devil turned round on you—where would you hide, Roper, the laws all being flat? This country's planted thick with laws from coast to coast—man's laws, not God's—and if you cut them down—and you're just the man to do it—d'you really think you could stand upright in the winds that would blow then? Yes, I'd give the Devil benefit of law, for my own safety's sake.[17]

Of course the devil—in this case, Cromwell—took the benefit of law without giving it back to More. Robert Bolt, who wrote the play, commented:

> If "Society" is the name we give to human behavior when it is patterned and orderly, then the Law (extending from empirical traffic regulations, through the mutating laws of property, and on to the great taboos like incest and patricide) is the very pattern of society. More's trust in the law was his trust in his society; his desperate sheltering beneath the forms of the law was his determination to remain within the shelter of society. Cromwell's contemptuous shattering of the forms of law by an unconcealed act of perjury showed how fragile for any individual is that shelter.[18]

We are all learning now in this country how fragile is the shelter of law. What if our poor young men in the mean streets won't obey it, our rich old men on Wall Street take advantage of it? Without God in our enlightened heavens, where will we derive our "values"? From the majority? From the brightest among us? From the most traditional? (Check Nazi Germany first.) We will finally be reduced to the poverty of our rationalism, which can only tell us something's wrong but give us no idea what to do about it.

(3) God's laws of life for persons, and indeed all creatures, are as immutable as the laws of the physical universe. Erazim Kohak is a philosopher at Boston University. For years he has lived close to the land in a simple house in a forest clearing in New Hampshire, "beyond the power line and the paved road." Kohak is not a romantic about nature, however. He knows the "natural" life can be "brutish and scarred by cruelty."[19] Kohak neither recommends some alternative, "more natural" form of life style nor a return of humanity to its pre-scientific origins. But he is profoundly convinced of the moral sense of nature, the evidence of God's hand in all living things. Humans have largely lost sight of that reality, Kohak says, blinded as they are by the lights of their cities and the brightness of their technology:

> We are still human, all too human; even amid our plastic gewgaws the moral sense of our being, the bond of love and labor, the vision of truth and justice, all remain constant. Yet that moral sense of our humanity is all too easily obscured by the mechanical order of our artifacts. Though no less there, it seems not longer evident to us as once it did to the Psalmist on a desert night. . . . In our daily lived experience, the starry heaven above and the moral law within have been heavily overlaid by artifacts and constructs.[20]

Human beings, especially those of the Jewish and Christian faiths, should be aware of their unique task as part of creation. Only the human stands at the intersection of time and eternity, able both to know the deep things of the physical laws of nature and to perceive the value of living things beyond their own lifespans. The celebration of the psalmist was nothing less than God's human creatures recognizing God's laws in the universe of life and rejoicing in their rightness and goodness. As Kohak commented,

> The glory of being human is the ability to recognize this pattern of rightness and to honor it as a moral law. The horror of being human is the ability to violate that rightness, living out of season—doing violence to the other, perverting the most sacred human relationships, devastating the world in greed, overriding its rhythm, not in the name of necessity and charity, but in the compulsion of coveting.
>
> What Judaism and its spiritual daughter, Christianity, sought to express in their commandments is the age-old, precious discovery of the rightness of life. Still, were those commandments no more than

that, their significance to the quest for the moral sense of life would remain marginal. It is not, because they are sanctified by the moral sense of nature in a second, deeper sense, not merely its rhythm but its rightness in eternity. Their common motif is the law of respect for the sacredness of being.[21]

Law once again becomes a key or meaning to life when we "moderns" recognize God's hand in all levels of life and assume our stewardship of its sacredness.

(4) *An understanding of God's law can never be separated from liberation.* Israel originally celebrated law—not the priestly punctilios, but the whole experience of God with humankind—in conjunction with God's deliverance of a poor slave people from oppression. The Law of God was always the law of freedom, of true liberty. Israel was not condemned to irresponsibility and chaos, as the "heathen" lived. The Law graciously gave the Israelites liberating guidance in their search for life. Bonhoeffer reflected on the liberation of the law in this way:

> When your son asks you in time to come, "What is the meaning of the testimonies and the statutes and the ordinances which the Lord our God commanded you?" then you shall say to your son, "We were Pharaoh's slaves in Egypt." . . . That is the answer to the question about the Law: God's deeds of deliverance, God's commandments and God's promise . . . God's law cannot be separated from his act of deliverance. The God of the Ten Commandments is the God who led you out of the land of Egypt (Exod 20:2). . . . "Yes, he loves his people; all those consecrated to him were in his hand; so they followed in thy steps, receiving direction from thee" (Deut 33:3).[22]

Jesus struck this same chord in his preaching of the reign or kingdom of God, life within God's truth. He found God's people again under oppression, as Moses found them in Egypt. This time they were bound by an ecclesiastical oppression as well as a political oppression, their feet cemented to the earth by the accretions of legalistic traditions. Jesus lived and died as a liberator from all such human tyranny. He called Israel to remember its past, as had the prophets, and to live in the freedom of that heritage. Nothing in any society is a more powerful social control than human laws masquerading as God's laws.

Allan Boesak, a South African preacher, wrote concerning the law of and freedom in Christ:

> Precisely because this people has been freed from the yoke of the pharaoh, precisely because the oppressive power of slavery has given way to the liberating and re-creating power of the righteous God, precisely because this space to know and hear him, to follow him, is now theirs—precisely for these reasons the people can be expected to use their new freedom to serve the Living One.
>
> We find the same thing in the law of Christ: it is framed by the reality, the mercy, the love of the Messiah himself. His life's work, his obedience, his liberative deeds are the content, the force, and the fullness of his law. The joyful truth of the Torah, and the joy over the differentness of this law, lies in the undertone: the liberator is the law giver.[23]

Bosak also commented on how Paul urged Christians to resist the legalizing forces that would once again place a "yoke of slavery" (Gal 5:1) about their necks:

> It is strange that Paul speaks of a "law." What does this mean? Is it not also in this letter [Galatians] to this same congregation that Paul argues against the slavish adherence to the Law, against legalism? The whole of chapters three and four deals with this theme of freedom from the Law, and chapter five begins with Paul's famous cry to triumph: "For freedom Christ has set us free; stand fast therefore, and do not submit again to a yoke of slavery."
>
> So when he now goes on to speak of a "law," it is clear that it—this "law of Christ"—is essentially different from the legalism he has just been warning against. In our text the Law is called "the law of Christ." And indeed it is his law; he enacted it and he carried it out. It was he who was willing to be mediator between God and humankind. It was he who through his passion and death became the reconciler, the agent of God's salvation for humankind. For the sake of humankind he became the bearer of a great burden: in his death on the cross he bears the sins of the world, our indolence, our unwillingness, our selfishness.[24]

The church of Jesus Christ must likewise be a church of burden-sharers, one with another, not burden-bringers. That means the clergy and priesthood must fight against society's dehumanizing and demeaning oppression of its weak and poor. But they must also stand against their own institutions' inevitable tendencies to seek wealth and power by magnifying human guilt and multiplying religious regulations. The keys of Christ are indeed for loosing and binding (Matt

16:19), but the life of Jesus makes plain which of those he considered his major task.

The "laws of the church"—or better said, the churches, since every Christian group has developed its own set of oral laws from its own tradition—are still and always "the laws of man." They are our interpretations of the gospel. Even with our best intentions, they are still ours. The early church had not left the first century before the inclusive spirit of Jesus, his most radical and yet characteristic hallmark, began to be reversed. Even Peter, Paul, and the later biblical epistle writers struggled against their own inclinations to adjust the gospel of Jesus to a less controversial posture.

At first Peter was all for admitting Gentiles to the church. But once back in the Jewish Christian center of Jerusalem, he gave in to the pressure to accommodate the new Christian message to Jewish law and ritual. Paul seemed to involve women heavily in his missionary work. But later the pressures of a Greek culture that for centuries had relegated "decent" women to a cloistered domestic existence seemed to cause him to trim his sails. Women could participate in the church, but in a secondary role. (Some New Testament scholars argue that these later restrictions do not match Paul's earlier attitudes and are in fact from the "deuteroPauline" authors, disciples who blended Paul's thoughts with their own.)

The church has been plagued with such loss of nerve throughout its history. It wants to be successful. After all, didn't Jesus command us to be victorious? (Actually, not; but that's another story.) So the church promptly enters into the best marketing strategy it can devise to persuade its neighbors that they should join up: the church is not really subversive of their culture, whatever it happens to be—liberal anythingism or fundamentalist know-nothingism—and it will support their "values," keep their kids in line, and generally not rock any boat they are paddling. (Today this is sometimes called the church growth movement.)

John Wesley was barred from preaching in some of his own churches because he endorsed women preachers. Wesley always assumed that women should preach, as well as men. After all, in the "free-church" tradition, the authority to do so came at Pentecost when women were also present and touched by the Spirit's universal descent, rather than through some "old-boy" system of male-clubby, secret handshake. Of course, as soon as Wesley died, the Methodists threw out that embarrassing women-preacher notion. (It wouldn't bring in members, you know. Some women didn't like it either.) Later on, Christians in the South found texts in the Bible to accomodate—nay, baptize—the slavery of their region. Cheap labor was essential to their cotton-picking economy, just as child labor was "vital" to the textile mills in England. And so on and so on.

Of course, the modern church growth movement doesn't favor slavery or the exclusion of women—at least not *per se*. It does, however, favor the "H.U." principle, the homogeneous unit principle. Simply put, this growth principle says that people like to join churches composed of members similar to themselves. ("Birds of a feather like to flock together," don't you know.) This common sense truth warns that it is off-putting to folks to be in the same pew with people who are poorer, or wealthier, or better educated, or less educated, or different in race or politics or social status from themselves. In other words, Jesus' notion of church hasn't got a chance. But the church growth movement says we can still build huge, wealthy organizations where we can get together with our friends and talk about Jesus and interpret his words so that they don't contradict anything anybody in our church does or believes in real life. Meanwhile, we can "convert" them to an assurance of heavenly bliss.

Our desire for success drives us into such tragic nonsense. The church growth movement feeds our prejudices by assuring us that we are commanded to reach the whole world, generally quoting the Great Commission: "Go into all the world and make disciples." It never notices that the emphasis of the commandment is for the church to be inclusive, not successful. Jesus emphasized that his all-Jewish followers were to go to every nation, race, and group, not just our own. Nothing is said about results. Who knows? Maybe Jesus really meant it when he said Christians were to be the small pinch of leaven in the loaf, not the large lump of dough.

Actually, the church growth movement has said very little to us that the devil hadn't already said to Jesus on the mount of temptation. Whenever the church has moved out of its minority quarters into majority status, it also has moved promptly out of the church house into the state house. Then it seizes advantages for itself from the state, which of course it pays for by crawling into bed with the prevailing government, whatever it may be. This principle has been true from

Law

Constantinople to Rome to Nashville. Compromises may make organizations grow, but they can never make the church grow.

The law of Christ is the law of liberation. No liberation can please masters as well as slaves, bless comfortable social structures as well as oppressed minorities. We—the church—cannot be both masters of the world and servants of Christ.

(5) *The words "literal" and "interpretation" can never be joined. One speaks of the letter, the other of the spirit.* In a valiant attempt to return to the faith of the early Hebrews, Israel pressed for strict adherence to the Law of Moses, the Pentateuch. The prophets soon saw the fallacy of their literalism. People were keeping the letter but not the spirit of the Law. God demanded that their external observances cease until their inward obedience began:

> What to me is the multitude of your sacrifices? says the LORD; I have had enough of burnt offerings of rams and the fat of fed beasts; I do not delight in the blood of bulls, or of lambs, or of goats.
>
> When you come to appear before me, who asked this from your hand? Trample my courts no more; bringing offerings is futile; incense is an abomination to me. New moon and sabbath and calling of convocation—I cannot endure solemn assemblies with iniquity.
>
> Your new moons and your appointed festivals my soul hates; they have become a burden to me, I am weary of bearing them. When you stretch out your hands, I will hide my eyes from you; even though you make many prayers, I will not listen; your hands are full of blood.
>
> How the faithful city has become a whore! She that was full of justice, righteousness lodged in her—but now murderers! Your silver has become dross, your wine is mixed with water. Your princes are rebels and companions of thieves. Everyone loves a bribe and runs after gifts. They do not defend the orphan, and the widow's cause does not come before them. (Isa 1:11-15; 21-23)

Amos likewise wrote in classic words:

> I hate, I despise your festivals, and I take no delight in your solemn assemblies. Even though you offer me your burnt offerings and grain offerings, I will not accept them; and the offerings of well-being of your fatted animals I will not look upon. Take away from

me the noise of your songs; I will not listen to the melody of your harps. But let justice roll down like waters and righteousness like an everflowing stream. (5:21-24)

But could not the words of Jesus or of Paul be lived literally? Eduard Schweitzer wrote:

> One must determine what represents the service of love concretely towards someone else and what represents evasion; literal fulfillment of the law of Jesus can no more relieve us of this decision than literal fulfillment of the Law of Moses. This point is made by the fact that the community again and again used new approaches to find out what Jesus' instruction meant in actual practice.[25]

Could any "literal" practice of the teachings of Jesus, as a law, fulfill the Spirit of Jesus for every century? Schweitzer continued:

> The limitations of all concrete efforts must be noted. Had Jesus established a new system of family or labor law in Palestine, it would be long outmoded and vanished; above all, in a different situation it would have proved to be as wrong as what it replaced, and under certain circumstances more dangerous. The law of the medieval church against interest, inspired directly by the Sermon on the Mount . . . meant that only the Jews could make commercial loans, with results that were totally pernicious.[26]

It is strange but true. All attempts to live a godly life on the basis of literalism are doomed to failure. To be truly "literal," one would need to live in the very time and place of the original commandment—indeed, to be those persons to whom such laws were given. Consider these words: "Women should be silent in the churches" (1 Cor 14:34); "I permit no woman to teach or have authority over a man; she is to keep silent" (1 Tim 2:12). Which church practices these commands literally? Do not women teach and sing and testify in virtually all churches? Only by twisting such "literal" words to mean that women should not preach in the pulpit of the church can the most literalistic of churches claim to obey them. (When a well-known female political figure recently preached the morning sermon at a fundamentalist church, they called it "giving her testimony.")

What about other words from the same passage of Scripture? "The women should dress themselves modestly and decently in suitable clothing, not with their hair braided, or with gold, pearls, or expensive clothes." (1 Tim 2:9). Has anybody enforced that one lately? Obedience to the spirit of Jesus requires interpretation of the meaning of such texts. In the Mediterranean world of the first century, words such as these meant that Christians should do nothing that would bring shame upon the church or keep out the less fortunate.

Those principles are valid today. But if these time-conditioned sayings are etched in stone for all time as the eternal order of God, what becomes of the inclusiveness of a Galilean who was followed by peasant women and children, strictly contrary to the male-female decorum of Jewish custom? How can we explain God's angel telling the women at the tomb to go to the male apostles to tell them of the resurrection of Jesus? How could God justify using women to proclaim (preach, teach) this "best news" to those who regarded themselves as owners of the sole distributorship for the Good News?

Paul wrote:

> Such is the confidence that we have through Christ toward God. Not that we are competent of ourselves to claim anything as coming from us; our competence is from God, who has made us competent to be ministers of a new covenant, not of letter but of spirit; for the letter [*gramma*, that which is written] kills, but the Spirit gives life.
>
> Now if the ministry of death, chiseled in letters on stone tablets, came in glory so that the people of Israel could not gaze at Moses' face because of the glory of his face, a glory now set aside, how much more will the ministry of the Spirit come in glory? For if there was glory in the ministry of condemnation, much more does the ministry of justification abound in glory!
>
> Now the Lord is the Spirit, and where the Spirit of the Lord is, there is freedom. And all of us, with unveiled faces, seeing the glory of the Lord as though reflected in a mirror, are being transformed into the same image from one degree of glory to another; for this comes from the Lord, the Spirit. (2 Cor 3:4-9, 17-18)

"All of us . . . are being transformed," if we are the church of Jesus: Peter concerning Gentiles, Paul concerning women, Southerners and South Africans concerning blacks, male preachers concerning women preachers. All of us, our faces, too, once veiled by the customs of "the fathers," now see the glory of the Lord and the grace of the law of Christ. "All of us . . . are being transformed," if always too slowly, "for this comes from the Lord, the Spirit." And "where the Spirit of the Lord is, there is freedom." This law unlocks doors to life.

Notes

[1] Dietrich Bonhoeffer, *Meditating on the Word,* ed. and trans. David McI. Gracie (Nashville TN: The Upper Room, 1986) 108-109, 116.

[2] *Theological Dictionary of the New Testament,* Gerhard Kittel, ed. (Grand Rapids MI: Eerdmans, 1967)4: 1044.

[3] Bonhoeffer, 112-13.

[4] J. I. Packer, "The Puritan Conscience," *Faith and a Good Conscience* (London: Morcott Press, 1963) 27.

[5] Ibid., 28.

[6] Ibid., 30.

[7] Ibid., 24.

[8] Babette May Levy, *Preaching in the First Half Century of New England History* (New York: Russell & Russell, 1945) 64.

[9] Edmund S. Morgan, *The Puritan Family* (New York: Harper and Row, 1966) 35.

[10] Ibid., 35-36.

[11] Kai T. Erickson, *Wayward Puritans* (New York: John Wiley and Sons, 1966) 57.

[12] Thomas Bray, "For God or for Satan," Dudley W. R. Bahlam, *The Moral Revolution of 1688* (New Haven CT: Yale University Press, 1957) 23-24.

[13] Levy, 59.

[14] Walter Bruggeman, *Finally Comes the Poet* (Minneapolis: Fortress Press, 1989) 65.

[15] Stanley Hauerwas, "Preaching As Though We Had Enemies," *First Things,* May 1995, 45-49.

[16] Eli Sagan, *The Honey and the Hemlock* (Princeton NJ: Princeton University Press, 1991) 32.

[17] Robert Bolt, *A Man for All Seasons* (New York: Random House, 1962) 66-67.

[18] Ibid., xvi

[19] Erazim Kohak, *The Embers and the Stars* (Chicago: University of Chicago Press, 1984) x, xii.

[20] Ibid., xi.

[21] Ibid., 84.

[22] Bonhoeffer, 107-108.

[23] Allan Boesak, *The Finger of God* (Maryknoll NY: Orbis Books, 1979) 64-65.

[24] Ibid., 64-65

[25] Eduard Schweitzer, trans. David Green, *The Good News According to Matthew* (Atlanta: John Knox Press, 1975) 205.

[26] Ibid., 208.

CHAPTER 4

THE SELF

The Fantasy Child and the "Real Me"

On August 20, 1977, an 1800-pound spacecraft was launched from Cape Canaveral to take advantage of a planetary alignment that occurs only once every 176 years. This rare alignment would allow it to conduct a grand tour of all the outer planets in our solar system except Pluto. *Voyager II* succeeded in its fantastic journey beyond anyone's imagination. The information gained from its probe has subsequently rewritten the book on our planets.

For example, *Voyager II* discovered live volcanoes on the Jovian Moon Io and revealed the amazing pallet of colors in Jupiter's raging atmosphere. Scientists also marveled at the revelation that Uranus, incredibly, had once been knocked off its axis by an ancient collision. Even familiar features of the planets, such as Saturn's rings, were shown to possess stunning complexity. All in all, enough information was sent back to earth to fill 6,000 sets of *Encyclopedia Britannica*. Yet someday this information will be regarded as a mere introduction to the complexities of our solar system.

Even so, we know far more about the physical universe than we do about that mysterious entity we call the self. So far as we are able to know presently, the self-awareness of humans is rarer than anything yet discovered in the universe's periodic table of elements. Somehow each of us stands at the center of a complex and unique set of feelings, observations, and experiences. We think of this complex center as our self. Billy Collins pondered the self in his poem, "One Life to Live":

> This is the only life I have, this one in my head,
> the one that travels along the surface of my body
> singing the low voltage song of the ego,
>
> the one that feels like a ball between my ears
> sometimes, and other times feels absolutely galactic,
>
> the life that my feet carry around like two blind
> scholars working together on a troublesome manuscript.

> This is the only life I have, and I am standing
> dead in the center of it like a man doing a rope trick
> in a rodeo, passing the lasso over his body,
> smiling inside a twirling of ovals and ellipses.
>
> This is the only life I have, and I never step out of it
> except to follow a character down the alleys of a novel
> or when love makes me want to remove my clothes
> and sail classical records off a cliff.
>
> Otherwise you can always find me within this hoop of myself,
> the rope flying around me, moving up to encircle my head
> like an equator or a halo or a zero.

The complexities of the self continually occupy psychologists, psychiatrists, and neurologists, and preoccupy the rest of us, leaving us with many questions. Who are we? How did we get this way? Why are we here? Does life have meaning? Specifically, what meaning, if any, does my life have? How am I distinctly formed and intended?

The sciences of the self, such as psychology, only began shortly before this century. Nevertheless, it is probably fair to say that no other topic in the twentieth century has held center stage longer than questions about the self. Some of us will spend much of our lives in counseling or therapy trying to unpack the nest of boxes that is ourselves. Some persons will focus on their birth parents and their effect on the person they've become. Others will try to understand the myriad influences of environment and culture on their behavior. Others will concentrate on making responsible choices to alter the person they've become into the person they'd like to be.

Anyone who has gone though even one hour of therapy knows what a foot-tangling, mind-confusing chase this can be. The scientists of the mind are divided into widely differing camps—to say the least. Anyone who has gone from one such doctor to another frequently feels like the fall guy in a tag-team wrestling match. In the short run, of course, most people come away from counseling helped with their immediate problems and enabled to cope better with life. But in the long run, many still continue to search for their true selves, the person they want to be, the "real me"—whatever that means.

"Know thyself" is good advice, as ancient as it is common. But how? Three possibilities confront me in this search for my true identity: I can be the child of my parents, the child my parents projected upon me; or I can allow someone else to be my parent, thereby becoming someone else's child; or I can be the child of my own invention, thus becoming my own parent. In fact, all of us do all three.

The Child of My Parents

As long as I live I will be inhabited by the child my parents wanted me to be, the child my parents projected upon me. Even if I consciously rebel against becoming that child and do the opposite of what they wanted, I'm still shaped by the image of the fantasy child of my parents. Like it or not, their fingerprints are indelible upon my mind, my emotions, my life.

A student once told me he was in great conflict with his father about his choice of a graduate school. His father wanted him to attend his old school, but the boy rebelled. In speech familiar to many parents, he told his father that he was tired of having to do as he said. He wanted to make his own choices. I agreed with the student. He should make his own choice of graduate school. So what was his problem? The school he really wanted to attend was also his father's school. He said if he went where he really wanted to go, his father would assume he had given in as usual and conformed to his wishes. He had to make a statement of his right to independence. But he felt miserable and trapped. If he chose another school, he wouldn't be going where he really wanted to go.

No wonder the student felt trapped! His father was still dictating his choices, only this time from the negative side. Until the boy could make the decision that was right for him, even if it was also his demanding father's choice, he would never be free of parental control.

That student was neither the first nor the last in a long line of parental puppets, some with head-nodding "yes" strings, others with knee-jerk "no" strings pulled by their parents. And you don't have to be young to have this problem. Our parents don't even have to be alive to pull our strings.

As I grew up, I always hoped to be taller than my six-foot father. I had every reason to hope so. Most boys were taller than their father by two inches, I'd been told. Every year my mother measured my height with a mark on the doorjamb beside the refrigerator. Every year, it seemed, I stayed about the same size while the refrigerator got taller.

Many of us grow up in someone's shadow, the shade cast by some tall oak in our world—a father, a mother, a successful sibling, a friend.

No matter what our accomplishments, we never feel we measure up to the stature of that person. Our best accomplishments still appear trivial to us; our least failures seem to diminish ourselves.

The biblical character Isaac had these shadows over him, and more. He was the son of a great father, Abraham, whom he would never exceed. When he had a son, Jacob, the Scripture became more interested in the boy than in the father. Isaac was never tall enough in the Bible, nor small enough, neither good enough nor bad enough, to be noticed. Isaac was merely respectable. He had only one moment in the spotlight. Early in his life his father bound him to an altar, and his life was nearly cut out of his body—all at the command of God. If there had been psychiatrists in Isaac's day, an army of them couldn't have gotten that trauma out of his mind.

But Isaac didn't die. He went on living an ordinary life. He suffered, as we all do, from the petty afflictions of day-to-day existence. The never-ending quarrels of his daughters-in-law made him want to put them on the first bus north, or else put himself on the first bus south. His sons, Jacob and Esau, despised one another. At the end of his life he died blind, deceived by his wife and younger son. All in all, Isaac's life sounds like a bit part for a minor actor in a soap opera.

If we look more closely, however, Isaac's life was anything but the life of a failure. In Genesis 26 God promised to bless him. In fact, God said that the promise to Abraham, that his children would be "as numerous as the stars of heaven" (v. 4), would be fulfilled through Isaac. Later Isaac also became rich. He owned flocks and herds "and a great household, so that the Philistines envied him." (v. 14). He had a knack for finding water in the desert, the equivalent in our time of a successful wildcatter in an oil field. First he unstopped the old wells that his father had dug, wells that later had been blocked with dirt by the Philistines. Then he dug new wells of his own. The first well he named "Contention," for his struggles with the Philistines. The second he named "Enmity," because of the enemies he made by digging it. But the third he named "Room," "Freedom," saying, "Now the Lord has made room for us" (v. 22).

Yet it was another incident that established Isaac's strong sense of self, the naming of his father's wells. Instead of renaming them "Isaac Number 1," "Isaac Number 2," and so on, he gave them their old names, the names his father Abraham had given them. Isaac must have been tempted to name those old wells for himself. After all, hadn't Abraham already gotten enough column-inches in the Old Testament? But he recognized the wells as his father's accomplishment and honored them with his father's name. You've got to be pretty secure to do that.

Only secure people can acknowledge the contributions of their parents to their lives. Insecure people readily talk about their parents' mistakes and the kinks those mistakes gave them. But their sense of self is so slight that they cannot attribute a single success to their parents. If it's good, I did it myself; if it's bad, my parents are to blame. How did Isaac become so secure? The names of Isaac's wells tell of his pilgrimage through life. In a way, they serve as his autobiography: "Quarrel" came first; "Struggle" followed; and "Room," or "Freedom" came last. Those names could be autobiographical for many of us also.

Quarrels with parental influence and the struggle for personal identity are typical of the growing-up process. But in order to get space, room, freedom in life, eventually we have to stop merely reacting against our parents. If we don't, we will never be our own person. Anyone who has to kick and step on mother and dad will always be a little person. If we can't eventually say I understand, we will always be insecure. We don't have to say that we agree—sometimes that isn't possible—but we do have to understand: I understand the harm done by your mistakes to my life, but I also understand the contributions you made to my life.

Franklin Jacobs, who was five-feet-eight inches tall, once jumped an incredible seven-feet, seven-inches in a track meet, nearly two feet above his head. He was asked how anyone so short could jump so high. He replied, "Tallness isn't measured in inches. It's determined by the state of your mind." If that's true, Isaac was a towering figure. His sense of self was undiminished by the accomplishments and powerful personalities of his parents. The first step in the discovery of our selfhood is the acknowledgement of the contributions of our past.

The contribution of place is also more powerful in our lives than we usually recognize. Winifred Gallagher published a provocative book, *The Power of Place*. In it she describes the influence of our surroundings—the places where we grew up and the places where we live—on our subsequent lives.

> Throughout history, people of all cultures have assumed that environment influences behavior. Now modern science is confirming

that our actions, thoughts, and feelings are indeed shaped not just by our genes and neurochemistry, history and relationships, but also by our surroundings.[2]

Individuals who can never come to terms with their backgrounds become one-sided and malformed. By denying that we are from some provincial section of the country or some little town that embarrasses us, we thrust ourselves into a life-long masquerade. We put on faces we think others will admire; we constantly comb our hair to be sure no traces of hay are left in it. We adopt manners, accents, and clothing to disguise our true origins. We may become angry, even enraged, if someone discovers our secret. Like Simon Peter on the night of Jesus' arrest, when our accent betrays us, we will deny that we know our old friends.

We play this game, too, about our religious ancestry if it embarrasses us. We deny the spiritual parents that gave us birth. We insist that not a trace of their influence remains in us. True, many of us outgrow our spiritual origins. Often we move away from the narrow and parochial environments of our childhood faiths. But to deny that those faiths made a contribution to us is merely to betray our insecurity. It also reveals a new but equally narrow and parochial vision. Gilbert and Sullivan once spoke of the man who admired "every age but this and every country but his own." That's no good. Freedom only comes to us when we can appreciate our rural parents or our kindergarten faiths, though we may have moved away into a religious life of our own.

Denominations and churches, too, should affirm such decisions. They should recognize that the development of the spiritual self sometimes requires a new home, new relationships, new opportunities for maturing. But letting go is no easier for them than it is for parents. Churches rarely show the modesty of John the Baptist. When his followers began following Jesus, John could say, "He must increase, but I must decrease" (John 3:30).

Someone Else's Child

To some extent, I am also the child of the invention of others. I do not have one set of parents; I have many parents. We all do. Significant relatives, teachers, peers—especially, our peers at a distance—our culture also gave birth to us. These parents frequently give birth to a person quite different from the fantasy child of our birth parents.

Some of this influence is good. Someone else may have given birth to your passion for music, your love for the outdoors, your political views, or even your religious convictions. Others may have given birth to hurtful habits and harmful ways. Some of these parents we know well, better even than our birth parents. But parts of our selves were engendered by persons we can no longer remember or whose names we never knew. Still other parents are completely anonymous and impersonal, the powerful social forces that shape our prejudices, wants, and deepest fears. Our understanding of ourselves is always connected to the influence of these birthing agents, too. Sometimes our entire life's direction is shaped by the opinions of these other parents. We want to become what people admire; we want to do what others think is worth doing. But what is that?

As a child, my nearest relative other than my parents was an older cousin who lived in my hometown. He always dreamed of joining the circus. Every year when the circus came to town, he and I would go to the fairgrounds to watch the circus employees set up their tents. To my surprise, one day he did run away and join the circus. Of course, he was forty years old, a geologist with a wife and children and an elderly mother living in their home. (To his credit, he did take all of them with him—and they loved it.)

Most of our ambitions are not so exotic, nor so definite. I still remember how surprised I was at the age of twelve when Herby, a friend of mine, told me he knew what he wanted to do when he grew up. "I want to be an undertaker," Herby said. He had an uncle who was an undertaker, and you could make a lot of money that way, the uncle had told him. Herby was an odd child, but I didn't know he was that odd. We were walking along a deep ditch that bordered a vast cotton field, and for a fleeting moment I hoped he wouldn't begin practicing his profession on the spot.

But what do you do when you begin your senior year in college, as do many of the students I teach, when "undecided" is still listed as your major? Even worse, what does it do to your self-image if you approach your forties or fifties still undecided?

Carl Jung once said that vocation is the link between the individual and society. If someone asks us who we are, how do we answer? Besides telling our name, we say what we do: I am an accountant with

IBM; I am a fifth-grade teacher at Westlake Elementary school. Many of the frustrations of unemployed women and retirees, their sense of loss of identity, can be attributed to society's fixation on vocation as the source of our identity. The self-help books tell you not to worry about what people think; just believe in your own worth no matter what you are paid or what your title is. But that isn't easy to do in a material culture like ours. It's even worse in some countries. The typical Japanese male "worker bee" has traditionally devoted his entire life, including his recreation, to his firm rather than his family or himself.

Reinhold Niebuhr once said that human beings always seek meaning in either solitude or society. Live beside Walden Pond, some say; there you will find yourself and find true meaning. Plunge yourself into the surf of society, others urge; join the information age. Get an education so you can get as good a job as possible and make as much money as possible and enjoy the most pleasurable life possible: that's society's formula for most of us these days. But can we find our true selves that way? At the end, when Herby, or somebody like him, puts us in the coffin, will our obituary resemble the person we wanted to be?

Sure, if you get rich enough you can live on an estate or in a gated subdivision with security devices on every window and door. Or, like Marlon Brando, you can own your own island. Or, like Michael Jackson, you can live as a semi-recluse in a secluded mansion. Or, like billionaire Howard Hughes, you can totally withdraw from human society to protect all of the wealth you've accumulated and take drugs until you're a vegetable. Did wealth beyond their wildest dreams lead them to their true selves? Ironic, isn't it? Famous personalities push their way to the front of the line to be seen, to be known, to be famous. Then when they get famous enough, they refuse to give autographs and wear disguises when they go out in public, and sometimes they die alone and afraid without any sense of who they are.

Jesus told a parable about a rich fool who had accumulated everything he wanted in life and then congratulated himself. "Take it easy," he said to himself, "you've worked hard and scored big." Jesus said, "He talked like that to himself." Of course he did; there was nobody else to talk to. Jesus called him a fool, but mortality terminated his foolishness.

The church, too, has stumbled over this question of self-worth. Like the rest of us, the church has vacillated between the two poles of solitude and society. At first, the church advised solitude. The contemplative life was life at its highest, it said, and monks and nuns who pursued such a career practiced life at its purest. Personal development of individuality and the cultivation of the self were to be subjugated to the rules of the order and the choices of the church. Some seekers after God undoubtedly discovered themselves through this pursuit. Others, like Thomas Merton, raised profound questions about that way of life for the Christian self before God.

No one could say that Thomas Merton was not serious about the monastic life. In 1941 he entered a Trappist monastery at Bardstown, Kentucky. He earnestly believed that the way of silence, self-denial, and contemplation was the self's highest service before God. He didn't find that lifestyle easy. Living among the other monks irritated him. Again and again he requested permission to live by himself in a small, concrete house away from the quarters of the others. At last, with considerable misgivings on the part of his superiors, he was allowed to do so. Merton celebrated his absolute solitude at last.

But his writings, particularly *The Seven Story Mountain* (1948), increasingly made him famous. Visitors from all over the world came to talk with him, and Merton carried on constant correspondence with other theologians and thinkers. Eventually, as Monica Furlong wrote, his mind changed about many of his earlier ideas.

> What did it mean to be a monk, a contemplative, in the twentieth century? In a way his whole twenty-seven years at Gethsemani had been an attempt to find the answer to this problem, and as the years stripped away the obvious answers and the comforting illusions, he felt he was left with little but his humanity . . . He began to see the monk not, as he had believed in youth, as someone special, undertaking feats of incredible ascetic heroism for the love of God, but as one who was not afraid to be simply "man," who, as he lived near to nature and his appetites, was the "measure" of what others might be if society did not distort them with greed or ambition or lust or desperate want.[3]

For twenty-seven years he had sought to find the highest spiritual development of the self. To his growing wonder and excitement he began to realize that the pinnacle of true spirituality was to be "ordinary," to be fully human, "in the way that few human beings succeed in becoming so simply and naturally themselves."[4] Ironically, just before his unexpected death, he wrote these words:

> "Coming to the monastery has been for me exactly the right kind of withdrawal. It has given me perspective. It has taught me how to live. And now I owe everyone else in the world a share of that life. My first duty is to start, for the first time, to live as a member of a human race which is no more (and no less) ridiculous than I am myself."[5]

Thomas Merton, like Dietrich Bonhoeffer before him in a Nazi prison, came to regard solitude before God as only valuable for preparation for service to humankind. Both of these profound Christians learned that we are to turn inward only to turn outward.

Jesus himself was no ascetic. His periods of solitude before God were frequent. But when his disciples became overly fond of such spiritual camping, he told them to be up and going. "I have business elsewhere," he said (Matt 17:1-8; Mark 1:35-39).

Churches, whether Protestant or Catholic, invariably attempt to build homes on spiritual mountain peaks. To lose oneself in Zen-like contemplation; to immerse oneself constantly in spiritual retreats; to have prayers and devotions morning, noon and night; to speak the language of Zion in all conversations; to think of nothing earthly; to seek an ongoing emotional high in worship and life; to regard all amusement and pleasure and even art as frivolous unless religious; to live from the cradle to the grave in a ghetto-like colony of the society of the same (in schools, sports, friendships) in subdivisions of the same, where, as one songwriter put it, "Christian dogs chase Christian cats"—this is the ultimate escapist withdrawal of the church from society, even in the midst of our spiritually starving, secular culture.

The fears of worldly distraction that drove monks in the Middle Ages to their cloisters and the Puritans to their colonies are the same as those that threaten Christian participation in the world today. The true identity of the Christian, however, like that of Jesus, must be lived out in both solitude and society. We are to "come apart" with him to see God's way more clearly. But then we are to rejoin the masses of human beings in our world, no different from ourselves, except that we know we have been embraced by the loving grace of God.

The church, too, is a part of society. Like us, it also has multiple parentage. Its birth was certainly not virginal. Sometimes the church is the child of God; sometimes it is the offspring of secular culture. For any church today to embrace notions of a narrow, self-serving spirituality while favoring social theories that only better our class or clan, is to ride in the limousine of secularity with a "Clergy" sticker on its bumper. On the other hand, churches that have severed any meaningful connection with the demands of the gospel of Jesus and embraced the vague, vapid cliches of American "anythingism"—our happy new religion—are riding in the same vehicle with a different driver (its bumper sticker: "Faith Happens").

Just as you and I cannot escape the influence of our birth parents and genes, neither can we escape the molding fingers of our society. Yet only as human beings within our society, but not of our society, can we find and fulfill our true selves in the only time that God has given us.

My Own Child

The pressures of parents from one side and the pressures of society from another side drive us in yet a third direction. Most of us don't want to be the fantasy child of our birth parents. Nor do we want to be merely society's child, whether that society is secular or religious. We want to be our own child. Our deepest desire is to be what we want to be, to choose our own look and life. In short, we want to be our own parents. We want to give birth to ourselves.

Some of this desire makes sense. We can choose the traits of the fantasy child of our parents with which we identify. We can choose those habits and goals we affirm from our peer parents. We can adopt whatever attitudes or ambitions of society we believe best for us. Yet, even as we say such things, we feel the frustration and futility with which we struggle. How do I know which desires are mine and not those of my parents or my peers? Is that in fact possible? Do I exist as a human being, a self, apart from and other than these influences? Can I ever know my own mind? Is there even such a thing as "my own mind"? How can I know who I am?

My father was an Old South politician who prided himself on knowing everyone's name, or, at least, in making them think he did. It was astonishing how many names he did know. It was equally astonishing how many he didn't know but got away with. Do you remember me?" someone would ask. "Of course I remember you," he would say. And usually he did. But that didn't necessarily mean he remembered their name. And nothing would make him madder than for somebody to pin him down on the subject. "I'll bet you don't know who I am. Do you know my name?" someone would eventually ask. "No, I don't," my father would reply, his face getting redder by the minute. "And if you don't either, you're a hell of a lot worse off than I thought you were!"

A few generations ago people either "knew who they were," or something was mentally wrong with them. For most of the history of the world, one's self was defined by the family, the gender, the tribe. People in those days gave little thought to "who they were" or "what they would become." Serfs remained serfs; cheesemakers' children made cheese. John W. Gardner wrote concerning one's identity:

> In the stable periods of history, meaning was supplied in the context of a coherent community and traditionally prescribed patterns of culture. Today you can't count on any such heritage. You have to build meaning into your life, and you build it through your commitments—whether to your religion, to an ethical order as you conceive it, to your life's work, to loved ones, to your fellow humans. Young people run around searching for identity, but it isn't handed out free any more—not in this transient, rootless, pluralistic society. Your identity is what you've committed yourself to.[6]

The parlor game of "Who am I?" is still not enjoyed by most of the world. It is a pastime strictly for the privileged with plenty of alternatives to choose from and the leisure to reflect (or brood) on their lot. Today some of us go to incredible lengths to change ourselves into the selves we wish we were. Consider, for example, these cases.

At age sixty-five Lydia Falcon had cosmetic surgery. Not a face-lift, nor a tummy tuck, nor breast implants—Lydia Falcon had calf implants (no, not young cows) for her skinny legs. "I just wish I'd done it earlier," she said. Anne Lamkin, an operating room nurse, had the same procedure. She got "the fuller legs I'd always dreamed of" and got rid of her tummy bulge at the same time. Her cosmetic surgeon liposuctioned fat cells from Anne's abdomen and put them in her calves. She lost three inches from her waist, and her once-skinny legs, according to her own account, became "slender but curvaceous." (Of course, every time she passes a Mrs. Fields' Cookies store, her legs drag her inside.)

Whether or not these ladies like themselves or not, their identity is the same. (Lest anyone should think this is merely female vanity,

The Self

calf implants began with male weight-lifters.) Life would be much simpler if shifting the shape of our calves was all we had to do to become satisfied with ourselves.

The greatest desire of the young is to "find themselves," so they can "be what they want to be." But isn't that reasoning in a circle? Can people be what they want to be until they find themselves? On the other hand, can they find themselves until they become what they want to be?

This is the great myth of self: inside me somewhere, unseeable by X-ray or even an MRI examination, is a stainless steel ball, a little sphere that contains "the real me." If I can encounter the right guru, or read the right book, or say the right mantra, or meet the right person—or something—I can unlock this secret sphere, and my true, pristine self will emerge. And once found, of course, this self will lead me aright, ever onward and upward to the Mountain-of-Where-I-Want-to-Go.

Sounds silly, put like that, doesn't it? But some such theory underlies not only the thinking of many students but also that of a large number of scientists of the mind, authors of betterment books, and spiritual savants of a thousand sorts. This myth of the self, however, contains a fatal presupposition. The self is no static entity. There is no "finding" the true self because it isn't sitting somewhere waiting to be discovered. The "real you" was not innate at birth, like your future height or the color of your skin. The self is constantly in process. It is changing and malleable. As John Gardner said, your identity is what you commit yourself to.

Many people feel well-adjusted as soon as they discover what they enjoy in life. Then they believe they have found themselves. Once they discover what they enjoy, they live it relentlessly. People who like to be in charge take charge of everyone. Those who love money get it any way they can, regardless of society's conventions or ethics. Other people believe they are truly themselves when they feel free enough to express their "true" feelings. I have known people who sincerely hated blacks, Jews, assertive women, men with long hair, and anyone from Texas, and didn't mind saying so to anyone. Is that the real me, the true but bigoted self, "warts and all," that I'm suppose to affirm and inflict on society? Is this my only option?

A Child of God

The Old Testament is the story of the people of Israel. They called themselves the children of God. But as they journeyed with God, those children were constantly relearning who they were. Amos said that God took Israel by the hand like an infant and led it in its toddling steps. As God did for the unstable Jacob ("the trickster"; the one who trips everyone up) who became Israel ("God rules"), God reinterpreted for the Hebrews who they were. Again and again in the Old Testament, God audaciously gave people new names as a symbol of their new selves.

Jesus likewise reinterpreted names to bring out the potential selves he saw in persons. "You are Peter, and on this rock I will build my church" (Matt 16:18), he said to Simon BarJonas ("son of Jonah"). In each of these cases, the focus of the renaming process was not on human psychology but on the transforming nature of an encounter with God.

I believe our understanding of the self needs similar reinterpretation. Unless we discover God's reality about selfhood, we will exhaust ourselves in the never-ending game of pursuing the elusive self. We could spend our whole lives in aimless and rotating choices of different selves, multiple parents, and various births.

Jesus explained it like this to the Pharisee Nicodemus: you must be born again. Of course, that diagnosis only confused Nicodemus, just as society and much of the church is confused by the saying today. Everyone is born twice, Jesus said, once from below and once from above. Why should you be astonished at that? he asked.

Conventional wisdom has it that being "born again" is a kind of second blessing, an advancement in rank for a Christian. "Born again" Christians are those who are somehow superior because they have had a mystical experience, generally an emotional one, that has made them some sort of superChristian. At least, that's the way society generally sees it. But Jesus said to Nicodemus,

> No one can see the kingdom of God without being born from above [born anew]. What is born of the flesh is flesh, and what is born of the Spirit is spirit. Do not be astonished that I said to you, "You must be born from above." (John 3:3-7)

In other words, being "born again" is not a spiritual merit badge. Every Christian is a person who has been born again, or anew, from

The Self

above. We have two births. We are all born once "of the flesh." That is, we are given birth once by our birth parents and heredity, the infinity of our generations; but that birth "of the flesh" also includes the birth parents of our environment, our society, our peers. That is the birth from below, the natural birth. We think what our society thinks; we hold the prejudices and prides our birth deals us.

We also need to be born anew, a second birth from above, a birth of the Spirit. That birth, Jesus said, produces a quite different self from that born of the first birth, the self from below. Like the wind, Jesus said, the Spirit of God is free to move as it chooses, blowing away the false expectations of culture, the insidious intrusions of human selfishness and egotism, the confining walls of exclusiveness and pride. Only this spiritual birth from above allows us to become a part of the reign of God on earth, the reign of justice and mercy and love. The Spirit gives birth to the new self in Christ.

Society fails to recognize that everyone, "religious" or not, is born twice. We are all born once of the flesh of our parents and our culture. We hold their opinions as truth—in fact, as more than truth, as reality. Eventually we are born of another spirit, one that we choose. This second birth results from whatever we commit ourselves to—our ultimate, true, internalized values. We may deceive ourselves about our true commitment; we may say that we still hold the old values of mom and dad and God and country. But whatever we value—to make it plain, whatever we go after—that is our "born-again" self. No wonder Jesus said, "Do not be astonished that I said to you, 'You must be born again.' " Everyone experiences it. Christians are simply those whose second birth is from a different spirit than those of this age: the spirit of Jesus.

In that most human of beings, Jesus of Nazareth, in whose face we nonetheless are able to see the face of God, God has projected upon human consciousness another self. This is the vision of humanity that God had from creation. That self is made available to all born anew of God's Spirit. The apostle Paul first spoke of this new life available to us in Christ. "So if anyone is in Christ, there is a new creation: everything old has passed away; see, everything has become new!" (2 Cor 5:17). Ephesians likewise tells us "to be renewed in the spirit of your minds, and to clothe yourselves with the new self (*kainos*, newly made), created according to the likeness of God" (4:23, 24). This is the true self, the "real me" everyone seeks: the new person in Christ, born from above; like Jesus, fully partaking of humanity, yet led by the Spirit of God.

Even so, as followers of Christ we never lose the uniqueness of our parentage, both physical and cultural. This real, human self is to be steadily transformed by the Word of God. Our true self cannot be less human or more spiritual than Jesus. We are not to adopt some pseudo-spiritual identity in exchange for our pseudo-secular identity, one false face for another. God wants children, not clones of the latest spiritual type. As children, we will always be learning. As children, we will always be growing. And as children, we will always be struggling against inner doubts that we are indeed who God says we are. Nevertheless, we only find our true selves when we acknowledge the transforming parentage of God.

Perhaps Dietrich Bonhoeffer said it best for all of us who struggle to become the person God has declared us to be. He wrote these words from his Nazi prison cell:

Who Am I?
Who am I? They often tell me
I stepped from my cell's confinement
Calmly, cheerfully, firmly,
Like a squire from his countryhouse.
Who am I? They often tell me
I used to speak to my warders
Freely and friendly and clearly,
As though it were mine to command.
Who am I? They also tell me
I bore the days of misfortune
Equably, smilingly, proudly,
Like one accustomed to win.

Am I then really all that which other men tell of?
Or am I only what I know of myself?
Restless and longing and sick, like a bird in a cage,
Struggling for breath, as though hands were compressing my throat,
Yearning for colors, for flowers, for the voices of birds,
Thirsting for words of kindness, for neighborliness,
Tossing in expectation of great events,
Powerlessly trembling for friends at an infinite distance,
Weary and empty at praying, at thinking, at making,

The Self

Faint, and ready to say farewell to it all?
Who am I? This or the other?
Am I one person today and tomorrow another?
Am I both at once? A hypocrite before others,
And before myself a contemptibly woebegone weakling?
Or is something within me still like a beaten army,
Fleeing in disorder from victory already achieved?

Who am I? They mock me, these lonely questions of mine.
Whoever I am, Thou knowest, O God, I am thine![7]

Notes

[1] Billie Collins, *Questions about Angels* (New York: Morrow, 1991) 71.

[2] Winifred Gallagher, *The Power of Place* (New York: HarperCollins, 1994) 103

[3] Monica Furlong, *Merton: A Biography* (London: Collins, 1980) xviii.

[4] Ibid.

[5] Ibid., 187.

[6] John W. Gardner, "Personal Renewal," *The McKinsey Quarterly*, No. 2 (1991): 72-78.

[7] Dietrich Bonhoeffer, *Letters and Papers from Prison*, ed. Eberhard Bethge, trans. Reginald Fuller (New York: Macmillan, 1971) 347-48.

Chapter 5

WEALTH

When Life Is Rich

In 1960 two planes collided in midair over Brazil. Most of the occupants died. But in a well-documented story, Brazilian newspapers reported that one man fell more than 10,000 feet into a soft field and survived with only minor injuries. Curious interviewers asked the survivor what he remembered from the experience. "The only thing I remember from the fall," he said, "was that just before I hit, I remember feeling to see if my wallet was still there. I don't know why I did that."

We do, don't we? It's the survival instinct of the twentieth century. Even in the ultimate crises of life, our instincts tell us that security is in our hip pocket. A popular financial program currently advertised on television promises to teach subscribers how to "die rich." Even on our way into the ground, our greatest fear is that somebody else—principally, of course, the government—will get the wealth we've devoted our lives to. Die rich? At best, our heirs may become rich when we die, but all of us will be equally poor when the undertakers finally snap the lid down.

Wealth always has been regarded as the most essential key to the "good" life. "Money can't buy happiness," we are fond of saying. But it seems to buy enough of everything else that we are willing to take our chances on happiness. Most of us don't know what life would be like with plenty of money, but we'd sure like to find out. Persons with money don't know what life would be like without money, and they definitely don't want to know. For most people, life is defined by either the absence or presence of money.

The first and most elementary of human instincts is survival. The second, close behind it, is survival while having and doing anything you want. The quest for simple survival makes the infant cry when he or she is hungry; the quest for survival with total autonomy makes the two-year-old throw a tantrum when some big person says no. In the teenage years and beyond, arguing, bargaining, wheedling, and flattering may replace the tantrum. But the drive is the same: I want whatever I want. And if lying, cheating, using, even destroying—one way or the other—is necessary, well, you gotta do what you gotta do.

By these standards, persons such as billionaire Howard Hughes, who could hold his own with any product of the 1990s, were the most successful of humankind ever. Before he became a completely drug-addicted recluse in a solitary hotel room, Hughes was asked in an interview if he was happy. "Happy?" he replied. "Yes, I suppose so. I mean, as happy as any man with two billion dollars can be. No, I'm not contented. There are too many abridgements of my freedom."

Too little freedom? Howard Hughes? But that's the reason we all set out on this autonomous journey in the first place. Ironic, isn't it? Up to a point, money, power, and fame seem to increase our autonomy and freedom. Beyond that point, some mysterious law of diminishing returns sets in. We become a virtual prisoner of the things we've obtained. It's as if we've been climbing a mountain. Every hundred yards or so upward puts us higher than others, gives us prominence. But at some point we stand on increasingly lonely, rocky, ever-smaller plateaus, exhausted from the climb and lacking the normal oxygen of life that nourishes the creatures below.

At a slightly lower level of wealth-climbing on that mountain, but only slightly, the same phenomenon can be observed in entertainers and professional athletes. A teen with a guitar longs to take his garage band to Nashville or New York; a girl with a voice envies the group on tour; a boy who can dunk a basketball at age fourteen dreams of the NBA. Eventually these young people make it. The "big bucks" come. They buy a house for mama and a sports car for themselves. They love the attention, the fame, the cheers. And the money. Oh yes, they love that money.

So why do some famous personalities refuse to give autographs, avoid interviews, and take vacations where no one can find them? Why do some of them spend their spare hours seeking some cause worth supporting? Why are their private lives frequently a sideshow for the tabloids? And why do so many of these people in the limelight eventually get off the treadmill—sometimes on their feet, sometimes on their faces?

Somewhere in their quest for life's second basic instinct, survival with complete autonomy, they have met themselves coming back.

They have discovered that complete autonomy is a trap. Getting completely on top means depending entirely on the life-support systems of others. The simple fact is, wealth will not even take care of itself, much less take care of you. Real friendship, real love, real self-worth, real acceptance, real meaning in life—money can be at least as much of a hindrance as a help in finding these. Why does a surplus of money complicate human experience?

Have you ever stopped to think how anybody ever got more than somebody else in the first place? Society originally began to form itself around who had what. Individuals who had more muscles and more sons worked more land, killed more game, ate when others were hungry, and fought off those who wanted what they had. Some of these sinewy sorts also took the land next door and the stew in that pot. From these powerful families came the landholders, rule-givers, kings, generals, and judges. Armies were built from personal bodyguards and servants; small kingdoms became large kingdoms.

Long before the time of Jesus, the Golden Rule was well in place: he who has the gold, rules. "Aristocracy" and the "leisure class" grew from the powerful who had others under them to add to their wealth by their work. Soon the "haves" and the "have-nots" would be described by other, more politically correct terms: "lords" and "serfs," "landed gentry" and "laborers," "well-to-do" and "disadvantaged."

The situation was no different in the first century for Jesus and his world. Jesus belonged to the peasant class, as did almost everybody else. Of course, those in Israel who had varying degrees of wealth, though much less numerous, exercised disproportionate power over commerce, the state, and even religion. The aristocracy controlled the priesthood, and especially the high priesthood that could come from only a very few families. That office had been bought and sold for more than a hundred years before the birth of Jesus. Taxes from Rome were onerous, as they always were from Israel's captors. The temple taxes likewise squeezed even more sweat and blood from the peasant class, who stood at the bottom of the getting-line and at the head of the giving-line. The Jewish aristocracy was probably more afraid of the Jewish peasants than of the Roman legions in their country. With good reason, too. Only thirty years after the death of Jesus the peasants revolted against the wealthy, exactly as the Sanhedrin (the Jewish high court, controlled by the aristocracy) had feared in the time of Jesus.

These connections between the power and wealth of the few, the peasant class and the poverty of the many, and the envy and hatred between the two classes continued through each successive generation. "The poor you have with you always," Jesus said; and as one of them, he knew what he was talking about. Education, except for learning a trade, became a luxury of the rich—the rich males. Social classes hardened. "Upper" classes and "lower" classes knew who they were and what they had and couldn't have (which is where we started: the haves and the have-nots). Little wonder money has always been seen as the ultimate key to life.

The Church and Its Money

The reaction of the Christian church to money has been strange. On the one hand, it knows that Christ himself was poor, and that he said such odd and puzzling things as, "It is easier for a camel to go through the eye of a needle than for someone who is rich to enter the kingdom of God" (Matt 19:24), and "Take nothing for your journey, no staff, nor bag, nor bread, nor money—not even an extra tunic" (Luke 9:3). These words have prompted parts of the church at times to renounce wealth, embrace poverty, and even become mendicant monks.

On the other hand, the church has been eager to point out wealthy followers of Jesus, such as Joseph of Arimathea, as proof that a few camels in fact did squeeze through the needle's eye. Some interpreters looking for a larger door for the rich have suggested that the "needle's eye" was actually a low gate that a camel could go through only by kneeling. That's a pious but wishful interpretation completely without basis in fact. (Anyone familiar with the notorious balkiness of the ill-tempered camel could guess how long camel drivers would use a gate only a medium-sized sheep could pass through.)

More important, the church itself obviously did not (and does not) renounce wealth. Once given official status by Constantine, the church seized upon its new-found power to amass wealth the like of which few kingdoms enjoyed—and without having to pay taxes. Once the Roman Empire collapsed, the Holy Roman Church stepped in. State and church lines became blurred, pope replaced emperor, curia replaced senate, and wealth replaced poverty.

The church justified such activity as part of its "church triumphant" motif, a theme now seized as eagerly by Protestants as

Catholics. That is, the earthly Jesus was poor and defenseless, but the heavenly Christ is rich and powerful. In his earthly life Jesus may have emptied himself, as Paul said, "Though he was rich, yet for your sakes he became poor, so that by his poverty you might become rich" (2 Cor 8:9); but his true state was power and riches. Never mind that the riches promised to believers was the richness of salvation, and the "triumph" of the church was to be its life under the reign of God, the "kingdom" of God. Why wait? Heaven will be nice, but temporal power is now. The scorn of millions upon the "hypocrisy" of the church has focused most often on its schizophrenic message about wealth.

The rich and powerful in the church are not the only ones, of course, to blame for this state of affairs. When poverty was a fixed way of life for most Christians, their faith looked steadily to the riches of a future life. They consoled themselves, even in slavery, with thoughts of eventual justice in heavenly rewards. But as their economic conditions changed, so did their theology. Charlatans (Paul might call them "false teachers") promised poor Christians certain wealth, here and now, and instant heavenly healing if they became followers—and, of course, liberal givers. Others, less blatant, promised that God would "open the windows of heaven" and shower believers with earthly wealth if they tithed to the church.

One millionaire businessman in the 1950s was invited to countless churches to "give his testimony" about how his wealth resulted directly from his tithing. Pastors who seriously doubted this jackpot-theory of tithing nonetheless kept their mouths shut, deciding that it helped their church budgets. And besides, who knew? Maybe it did work that way for some. (In an interesting side note, this particular millionaire's church ministry went somewhat into eclipse after an entire congregation of poor Scottish Baptists got up and walked out when he told them they would be rich "if they were faithful.")

The only thing suspect about money in most American churches today is whether they can get enough of it to keep their doors open. Once again those with money have formed an elite class, this time in churches and denominations. Only a courageous and exceptional pastor can contradict the church's wealthiest patrons. Usually he or she will be given the opportunity to minister elsewhere for forgetting the Golden Rule: "he who has the gold, rules."

Nor does this intimidation by wealth apply to mere church polity. Most especially it applies to sermons that contradict the politics of wealthy members or challenge how they make their money. "Liberal" politics is virtually dead in mainline Protestant churches (it was always virtually dead elsewhere), not because the theology of those churches has changed, but because the social and economic standing of their members has changed. (That old evangelical worthy, Charles Haddon Spurgeon, was a member of the Liberal Party in England.) As in first-century Israel or in feudal states, persons who have social control today intend to keep it to "conserve" their privileged way of life. (Sharing that way of life never seems to occur to them; or if it does, it is quickly dismissed as a radical idea.)

The South, so conservative in other ways, produced what some regard as the first piece of radical social legislation in this country, the Bankhead cotton act. This federal legislation gave economic protection to the region's cotton farmers. "Liberal" quickly becomes "conservative" if our way of life needs conserving. "Standing on your own two feet," without government help or interference, is the most widely-held religious doctrine south of the Mason-Dixon line—unless, of course, you want high tariffs to protect the cotton mills and clothing industry, or farm subsidies and price supports for sugar or peanuts, or restrictions on oil imports, or government grants for space research or super colliders, or bail-out relief for bankrupt banking and insurance companies, or tuition vouchers for private Christian schools. There are, you see, a few exceptions.

Old Southern preachers, long accustomed to endorsing populist policies while tip-toeing gingerly around social and economic sensitivities such as race (and perhaps tobacco and whiskey, depending on the state), suddenly found themselves in the New South faced with bewildering changes. Earlier, the churches of these pastors were filled with 85 percent or more who made their living, directly or indirectly, from farming. Most of them were literally dirt-poor. Now technicians, middle managers, corporate officers, and perhaps a few old-money landowners fill the same pews, the children and grandchildren of the dirt farmers and small shopowners.

The attitudes of the New Southerners on race, generally, would be regarded as liberal, even intolerable, by their grandparents in the faith who needed racial dominance for the cheap labor essential to their labor-intensive farming economy. On the other hand, the New Southerners' opposition to farm subsidies and "illegal aliens" (today's source of cheap labor in the fern and fruit industries in Florida, as well as the source of nannies for high-placed government officials in Washington) would have caused their elders to offer them a free ticket north on the next train.

Of course, the more economically conservative views of these New Southerners is nothing less than the same law of religious economics practiced by their ancestors: if it's good for business (make that, "bidness"), it can't be bad. Christians of this persuasion believe "trickle-down" theories of economics not only apply to economic prosperity but also to human well-being. That is, economic "mercy-drops"—tax relief, investment credits, capital gains benefits, and so on—which benefit those businesses and individuals on top of the economic hill will eventually "trickle down" to the peasants and their standard of living below. (This assumes, of course, that the peasants don't get tired of the mere trickle and decide to run up the hill and open the floodgates—and a few veins—in the process.)

This wistful theory of the rich certainly didn't prove true during the Middle Ages or the Industrial Revolution, nor when the so-called "robber barons" of American industry controlled all of the railroads and steel mills. Andrew Carnegie is remembered for two things: giving libraries to open the minds of people in many American cities and hiring goon-squads to crack the skulls of workers on strike against the starvation wages of his steel mills that paid for the libraries. If this be "trickle-down," let us make the least of it.

Some economists and numerous politicians claim the effectiveness of trickle-down economies, at least in theory. But it is hard to see how any Christian could argue for a trickle-down theory of human welfare. Such a belief naively assumes that by further concentrating money and power at the top of society, all individuals in that society would be bettered. True, eventually enough common laborers reading enough books in Carnegie's libraries would lead to their intellectual betterment (assuming they could read in the first place, a big assumption). But then what? Would they be content with their lot and that of their children? Or would they insist that wealth from their labors be less concentrated in the hands of a few families? And would they then support the government and the church that favored the rich and told them to meekly accept their lot in life?

It hasn't worked that way historically. Latin America rebelled against the oligarchies that controlled the governments and the church that amassed wealth and landholdings under them. Revolutions that overthrew monarchies in Europe and elsewhere always rejected Christianity, because it was identified with the causes of the wealthy. When Father Massillon, court preacher to Louis XIV, urged the French nobility to set aside a percentage of their income for the poor lest the nation fall in ruin, he was mocked. Yet that sermon came just eighty years before the storming of the Bastille by the French peasants. Only land reform in the United States and toleration of labor unions likely prevented widespread economic upheaval in this nation as in others.

The founders of the social gospel movement, the most demonized of all Christian liberals, dared to challenge the "let-them-eat-cake" theories of industrialists such as Carnegie. Washington Gladden, (1836–1918), a Congregationalist minister, became sensitized to the plight of the laboring class during his work in North Adams and Springfield, Massachusetts. Walter Rauschenbusch (1861–1918), a Baptist pastor and professor, cut his teeth on economic issues during his eleven-year ministry in New York City's "Hell's Kitchen" (the original "West Side Story"), the worst of the pockets of hopeless poverty in New York. He worked tirelessly against the injustices and social evils surrounding his parish, until he felt he was treating the symptoms but not the cause of these ills. Convinced that individual piety and good works alone could never correct the systemic wrongs he saw, Rauschenbusch spent the remainder of his life urging Christians to apply the gospel to the larger structures of government, industry, and wealth. Here is his paraphrase of 1 Corinthians 13:

> If I create wealth beyond the dream of past ages and increase not love, my heat is the flush of fever and my success will deal death.
>
> Though I have foresight to locate the fountains of riches, and power to preempt them, and skill to tap them, and have no loving vision for humanity, I am blind.
>
> Though I give of my profits to the poor and make princely endowments for those who toil for me, if I have no human fellowship of love with them my life is barren and doomed.
>
> Love is just and kind. Love is not greedy and covetous. Love exploits no one; it takes no unearned gain; it gives more than it gets. Love does not break down the lives of others to make wealth for itself; it makes wealth to build the life of all. Love seeks solidarity; it

tolerates no divisions; it prefers equal workmates; it shares its efficiency. Love enriches all, educates all, gladdens all.

The values created by love never fail; but whether there are class privileges, they shall fail; whether there are millions gathered, they shall be scattered; and whether there are vested rights, they shall be abolished. For in the past strong men lorded it in ruthlessness and strove for their own power and pride, but when the perfect social order comes, the strong shall serve the common good. Before the sun of Christ brought the dawn, men competed, and forced tribute from weakness, but when the full day shall come, they will work as mates in love, each for all and all for each. For now we see in the fog of selfishness, darkly, but then with social vision; now we see our fragmentary ends, but then we shall see the destinies of the race as God sees them. But now abideth honor, justice, and love, these three; and the greatest of these is love.[1]

To the surprise of many critics, Gladden and Rauschenbusch were deeply evangelical and pietiestic. Gladden wrote the well-known hymn, "O Master, Let Me Walk with Thee." Rauschenbusch was a fervent revival preacher. And Niebuhr was the author of the best-known prayer in America, now on plaques in every souvenir shop in America, the so-called "Serenity Prayer":

God, grant me the serenity to accept the things that cannot be changed. Grant me the courage to change the things that ought to be changed. Grant me the wisdom to distinguish one from the other. Amen.

Serenity, however, in these "New Age" days, is a good deal more popular than courage. Niebuhr likely would have called it a prayer for wisdom, if anything. And if he had all the royalties from the assorted goods carrying those words, he would have a personal problem of wealth to contend with.

The Golden Eighties

The decade of the 1980s has been roundly damned as a notorious era of preoccupation with money. In his 1989 book, *Circus of Ambition: The Culture of Wealth and Power in the Eighties,* John Taylor said that "the money culture" set the tone for the nation in those years. A popular television ad in Texas by an oil service company—now bankrupt

—concluded with a beautiful Dallas-cheerleader type saying, "And if you don't have an oil well, get one!" (A lot of working-sorts in Dallas would have liked to throw her off a derrick.)

Junk bonds, Michael Milken, and takeovers became buzz words. The stock market went on an upward rampage as taxes were cut while spending was not. The national deficit exploded. Staid old institutions such as banks and savings and loans sought go-go investments. Extravagance became the badge of success.

When Lawrence Tisch's son married Saul Steinberg's daughter at a ceremony at the Metropolitan Opera, they were surrounded by 50,000 French roses (so much for "buying American"). The wedding cost a cool three million. As Susan Gutfreund, wife of the chairman of Solomon Brothers moaned, "It's so expensive to be rich."

Michelle Osborn, wrote in *USA Today* (November 8, 1989):

> In the '80s, making money was the only standard of success. Eerily enough the decade's closest relative was the 1880s, known as the Gilded Age. Vernon Parrington said of that period: "Freedom had become individualism and individualism had become the inalienable right to pre-empt, to exploit, to squander. Gone were the old ideals along with the old restraints."

Every section of American culture, including the church, found itself competing to be the most popular, the most successful, the biggest, and therefore the most attractive to the public. The sharp eye of Annie Dillard observed:

> An intriguing entomological experiment shows that a male butterfly will ignore a living female butterfly of his own species in favor of a painted cardboard one, if the cardboard one is big. If the cardboard one is bigger than he is, bigger than any female butterfly ever could be. He jumps the piece of cardboard. Over and over again, he jumps the piece of cardboard. Nearby, the real, living female butterfly opens and closes her wings in vain.[2]

Certainly one of the primary preoccupations of the 1980s was to get as much money as possible while giving away as little of it as possible. Entering the 1990s, we were told naively by media authorities that the era of conspicuous consumption had come to an end. (Why, exactly, national characteristics, such as fashions, are supposed to change or even reverse every decade is unclear.) So far, besides a lot of finger-pointing at the past, this decade seems to be little different from the last one.

In fact, precisely such an optimistic prediction for less greed was made for the 1980s in 1974. Professor Amitai W. Etzioni of Columbia University was quoted at length in a *Wall Street Journal* article entitled, "Getting off the Treadmill" (April 12, 1974). According to Etzioni, Americans in the 1970s have grown tired of the "earning-spending ethic . . . working hard and consuming hard." They have no joy in living, he said; they are questioning their purpose in life, which "thus far has amounted to the production of resources during working hours and the consumption and destruction of them in leisure time." Obviously, however, the 1980s didn't get us off the treadmill of "working hard and consuming hard," except for speeding up and throwing a few of us off.

But does such larger social action concerning wealth, some "social gospel," have its place in the Christian movement? Shouldn't we content ourselves to help our own neighbor, our own neighborhood? At most, perhaps our own town? Beyond these limits, don't systems become too complex, too expensive, too wasteful? And politically, too divisive for the church?

Jesus seriously stretched the concept of the neighbor in his own time with his parable of the "Good Samaritan." The Jew was not regarded as "neighbor" to the Samaritans, no matter what their physical proximity. Likewise, Jews expected no neighborliness from Samaritans and gave none. The social barriers Jesus demanded to be overcome in those days rival the worst of our enmities today.

The fact is, we Christians cannot properly use our wealth unless we also stretch our definition of neighbor. For ourselves, as well as for the neighbor, and even for the world, we must reach out beyond those near us and like us. We may disapprove of the way our government seeks to solve such problems or the way in which their plans are managed or mismanaged. We have the right and the duty to change those plans or change that administration. But we do not have the right to use poor government as an excuse to mask our own under lying prejudice, indifference, selfishness, or greed. Walter Brueggemann wrote:

> Restlessness and greed are normative ways in the world, but they are acts of unfaith. It is given to us in the gospel to know that another way is possible and mandated, both in the public arena and in our closer lives.

Wealth

Jesus is the one who yielded in trust and obedience. He had all things given to him, but he did not grasp. He did not covet power for himself. Indeed, he did the very opposite. He emptied himself instead of seeking greater fullness. He emptied himself in great risk and at great cost (Phil 2:6-8). In response to his obedient emptying, God gives to him gifts: power for life, authority in the world, entry to the very rule of God (Phil 2:9-11).[3]

Whatever else Americans possess in the twentieth century, it should be obvious to all of us that the key to understanding wealth is not one of them. The gospel of Jesus, in spite of the strange twists given to it over the centuries by the church, nonetheless can point us to true wealth. Yet three questions call for answers. Are things unimportant? When is enough, enough? How can we get ahead without getting behind?

Are Things Important?

All the world's religions, not just Christianity, have tended to answer this question with absolutes: absolutely yes or absolutely no. Early monasticism and Christian asceticism were ways of saying no to material possessions. Those movements cited certain sayings of Jesus to his disciples, such as to "take no money" on their journeys about Galilee and to "deny oneself" and follow him. They recalled that he himself owned only a cloak, so far as we know, and "had no place to lay his head." Their vows of poverty stressed the negative effects of possessions on the Christian life.

At least as much of this emphasis on self-denial, however, came from Greek philosophy as from Christian gospel. According to some Greek thinking, the material world was evil. This view also included the human body, "the flesh." Only the soul—whatever that was—or the spirit was pure. When Paul referred to "false teachers," he was usually referring to some variety of a Greek philosophy called Gnosticism. For Gnostics, matter was evil, and only secret knowledge (possessed, of course, by them) could enlighten and liberate their followers. For that reason docetic Christians did not believe that Jesus had a real body, or that he died. He only appeared, or "seemed" (the meaning of *docetic*), to be human and to die.

Hebrew religion, to the contrary, was quite material. The human being was an animated body, not a pure soul trapped in an evil body of flesh. The Gnostics understood spirit as the breath of life that animated the body, but the two were inseparable parts of living persons. In the Hebrew language, spirit, breath, and wind are all the same word (*ruach*). God "breathed" on Adam and he lived. In Ezekiel's vision of dry bones, God asked "Mortal, can these bones live?" (Ezek 37:3). Only when God breathed upon them did the inert bodies on the ground come to life.

The Greeks at Athens ridiculed Paul's preaching of the resurrection. Another body was the last thing a Greek wanted. Gods had no real, fleshly bodies; that was their advantage as gods. When the soul escaped the cage of flesh like a bird, a pure and painless life became possible.

Once the body itself is evil, philosophically, then everything that the body demands for itself—its appetites—also become evil. Paul fought constantly against the notion that certain foods were evil, that "food and drink" were indicators of spirituality or the lack of it. Jesus himself said, "It is not what goes into the mouth that defiles a person, but it is what comes out of the mouth that defiles" (Matt 15:11). Of course he was judged "a glutton and a winebibber" (Matt 11:19, KJV) by those who shunned such "worldly" enjoyments. True, excess was warned against in both Old and New Testaments. But things in themselves, the material part of life, were never regarded as corrupt.

For example, when Jesus was teaching his disciples to depend upon God, he pointed to the flowers of the field and the birds of the air. They plainly receive what they need from beyond themselves. But human beings tend to overlook that about themselves, or even deny it. Yet birds eat and flowers drink. The "body" of flowers is beautiful, not evil and deceptive, something material that distractingly allures somber Christians from ethereal contemplation. Jesus said to his disciples about the material needs of life, "Your heavenly Father knows that you need all these things" (Matt 6:32). Yet he was also most clear that "one's life does not consist in the abundance of one's possessions" (Luke 12:15).

Therefore, *things* in themselves, are not the source of evil in the life of the Christian. The test of life comes from possessing those things. Most Christians (with notable exceptions) have become aware of the goodness of the created order. But money—"filthy lucre"—is still suspect. After all, "money is the root of all evil." Or is it?

That translation misses the point (and a few words). "The love of money can be found at the root of *all kinds* of evil" would be more accurate (1 Tim 6:10, my translation). Money itself does not give birth to evil. But all kinds of evil have occurred because of the love of money. Jesus warned the rich that they may become so possessed by their money, so preoccupied with it, so deceived by its seeming security, that camels can go through needles' eyes more easily than they can find God's way. That leads us to the second question concerning wealth.

How Can We Get Ahead Without Getting Behind?
If wealth is so risky and distracting, shouldn't we avoid it altogether— or at least, as much as possible—living on bare necessities? Are not those Buddhists right who regard striving as the root of all evil? Wealth comes by striving, for the most part. Isn't any effort at "getting ahead" a mistake?

For a number of years I ministered to a congregation composed largely of employees of a major electronics manufacturer. Compared with Mr. Ford's early workers about whom Niebuhr spoke, these people were well paid. The workers on the line—those who assembled the components—worked fixed hours and were paid accordingly. But farther up the corporate ladder, managers had no set hours, only set responsibilities. The company didn't care if upper managers came in late or left early as long as the assignment was done on time. They also didn't care if employees worked nights, weekends, and holidays, in the car or plane while traveling, or in the hotel room after they arrived there. The managers' assignments saw to that. And after two years on the same assignment, one's work load was increased twenty percent to fill the time he/she had gained by becoming more efficient. That became a company "law."

Close to the top of the ladder, executives lived for, with, and often in the company. Their pay and perks were stupendous. Home life was something usually only their wives cared for. Only the most driven, intense, and sometimes coldly ruthless got to the very top. Of course, an employee could say no to the company. Usually, however, refusal to keep up the pace, to live exclusively how and where it demanded, meant getting frozen in place never to advance again. Then only those who could endure spending the rest of their working lives in some backwater job in a side office remained with the company. The others who said no started looking for work. They had stayed with the treadmill too long. They never thought it would ever go so fast.

On a climb in the Himalayas, a group of British climbers were frustrated by the slow pace of their local equipment bearers. So they promised to increase their pay for faster movement. After two days the bearers refused to climb. The climbers were furious and demanded to know why. Their interpreter explained: "They are afraid to go on. They say they must wait for their souls to catch up with them." Few corporations today can imagine the need for such soulish respite.

The slaves of the Romans in the copper mines of the Negeb were used the same way as the employees of some modern companies: maximum production every day, more added constantly to the quotas of the strong until the weaker among them fall out. Of course, every corporation isn't run alike. But to a greater or lesser degree, in business the Third Law of Profits is always in effect: profits are never high enough.

Masao Takenaka, professor at Doshisha University's School of Theology, Kyota, Japan, wrote:

> We live an increasingly hectic life, and we are busy with much business. The character for busy in Chinese writing, which Koreans and Japanese also use, literally means to destroy one's heart. If we are too busy, we forget what is most important. It is interesting that the same components of the character for busy are used to indicate forgetfulness. Both mean the destruction of one's heart.

Like all things material, getting ahead in itself is not the problem. It's how we get ahead, what it does to us and those about us, and what we lose in the process. Understanding what "getting ahead" really means is crucial. Is getting ahead earning more? Being in charge of more people? Owning more? But what of personal values? Relationships with husbands, or wives, too rapidly growing children? What of friendships that may be lost? Wonderful, happy times at a slower pace, if at a lower income? Could it be that sometimes getting ahead means not taking a promotion or a transfer? Could getting ahead mean continuing to work for a small firm rather than a big, prestigious corporation that pays much more?

Wealth 83

Time and again I have asked really happy people about their careers. Without exception they tell of a crucial decision in the past to get off the ladder of "success"—perhaps not to move to a distant state, or not to let their family business be merged into the mega-business, or not to join the faceless firm where only one associate out of ten is ever asked to stay on for partnership.

If "getting ahead" is reduced to a matter of mere dollars and cents, then ethics and eventually all human considerations are irrelevant. The human animal in search of nothing but "more" can be more dangerous to its world than the most savage creatures that ever walked, swam, or crawled.

The ancient Sabbath of the Hebrews was God's first line of defense against such dehumanization. Sabbatarian legalists, of whatever century, have made Sabbath observance a virtual joke in secular society. The Puritans had many good qualities, but their rigidity and petty Sabbath laws soured their children and their children's children on "keeping the Sabbath holy." But Brueggemann has written:

> The possibility of Sabbath rest means that the world is not marked by frenzy, precariousness, threat, or restlessness. God's sovereignty is so sure that even God can ease off daily management of creation and the world will not fall apart. The world has a life of its own with some sustaining power that God has assigned to it. The act of Sabbath is an act of remembering the liberation that permitted new life. On each Sabbath day, the Exodus will be enacted in a remarkable way. Your servants shall rest "like you." Hans Walter Wolff has suggested that the Sabbath is the great equalizer, for that day is a foretaste of the kingdom when all—great and small—are to engage in this most godlike activity of being at peace. . . .
>
> Sabbath means desisting from the frantic pursuit of securing the world on our own terms. In that ancient society, as in ours, the practice of acquisitiveness—whether of things, power, or leisure—constitutes resistance to Sabbath. . . . the Sabbath was a great line of defense against exploitation, to permit the humanization of public life.
>
> This torah command is a summons to let God be fully God for one day, so that our anxiety should not devour us.[4]

I once heard the late Kelly Miller Smith, eloquent and brilliant professor and preacher, say that only blacks in America could really appreciate the Sabbath. During their days of slavery, Sunday was the only day they could assemble or find rest. In the following decades of prejudice, only on Sunday could they "be somebody," with a position and a title of respect in their own churches. No wonder, Smith said, that you would never hear a prayer by one of the old church members without somewhere in the prayer hearing these words: "and of sweet Sabbaths, there shall be no end!" Try to imagine those words in a white congregation, many of whom barely tolerate Sunday as a somewhat boring interruption in a busy week.

But for the disenfranchised of the world, the Sabbath is a time of equality, humanity, acceptance, identity, and true rest. Sabbath does not merely bring the rest that comes from the cessation of activity. God's Sabbath brings the rest that comes from the deep peace of belonging to a human family of love and worth. Little wonder that the church has always grown fastest among the poor of the earth.

Our nation, too, must decide what getting ahead means. And it will never do so as long as Christians believe that getting ahead means coming out on top of every other nation on earth; cutting the shrewdest, sharpest deals economically for ourselves alone; and seeing to it that cheap labor stays that way. Does getting ahead mean discount stores and others closing a blind eye to virtual slave labor or dehumanizing child labor abroad so that our company can always offer the lowest prices, always? Textile mills once allowed sub-human working conditions for children, because of low costs. Both England and the United States almost lost their souls until "radical" Christian voices told us that the bottom line is never the bottom line.

"Costly" can be defined in many different ways. Believe it or not—and the vast majority of moderns, even Christians, prefer not to believe it—sometimes making less money is the least costly way for a business, a nation, or a family wage-earner to truly get ahead. Unfortunately, it is usually late in the lives of individuals or nations, sometimes too late, before they realize how costly their prosperous way of living has been. As Robert Penn Warren wrote in "Fear and Trembling,"

> Can the heart's meditation wake us from life's long sleep,
> And instruct us how foolish and fond was our labor spent—
> Us who now know that only at death of ambition does the deep
> Energy crack crust, spurt forth, and leap
> From grottoes, dark—and from the caverned enchainment?[5]

Church and synagogue alike must redefine "getting ahead." Our unbridled lust for absolute autonomy in our nation means the destruction of human values. Ultimately, it will mean the destruction of human society itself. The Sabbath, now nearly lost, is God's great sign of the worth of the human life. Jesus put it this way: "The Sabbath was made for humankind, not humankind for the sabbath" (Mark 2:27).

Yet a final question remains. If the material part of life is not immaterial, and it is possible to get ahead in the true sense of the term without getting behind, then when is enough, enough? That seems to me to be the crux of the issue. How can we know when more money, another job or promotion, a larger house, or a more expensive "lifestyle" (to use a word that tells us part of the problem) would be a mistake? If the "bottom line" isn't the bottom line, what is?

When is Enough, Enough?

At one time, aborigines of the Australian Outback were said to count in this fashion: "one, two, three—enough!" Their way of life never promoted the need for more numbers. That might be a good idea for us as well, but it would come as quite a shock to the computer industry. We find it hard even to conceive of there ever being "enough," particularly enough money. The life and teachings of Jesus suggest two principles for knowing what "enough" is.

First, "enough" is too much when it destroys what you're trying to create. What is it we really want, anyway? When we Americans obviously are better off by far than most of the world, why our discontent, our restlessness, our constant craving for more of things? In the chapter on contentment I'll explore that question in some detail. At this point let me merely suggest that we are looking for comfort, but in the very broadest sense. We want the ease of security, peace of mind, and a deep-seated satisfaction. We want the sense of having attained something worthwhile. We want to know that those who come after us will not lack for those things, too.

How much money does it take to get there? The possible answers range from between none and an infinite, never-attainable number. We have already said that the Christian gospel rejects both of the extremes ultimate asceticism and infinite acquisition at times. Cults and sects of Christianity have given either answer. Early in Christianity, as we have seen, total renunciation was the romantically appealing answer, if relatively few practiced it. Today "getting from God" is the appealing answer, and it has many who preach and seek it.

In other words, many preachers teach that if we are faithful to God, we only have to let God know what we need and God will give it to us. "Faithful to God" in this sense generally means tithing to the church, or at least showing great generosity, and not practicing certain personal vices. (The list varies according to denomination, or even preacher). Strangely, larger ethical questions are never involved. For example, if "robber barons" of industry give generously to the church and haven't been convicted of a capital offense, they can become examples of God's reward to the faithful. It will not matter that their workers live in borderline poverty or work in flagrantly dangerous conditions. After all, they "created" jobs for the working class. Examples of such behavior among "Christian" capitalists of both England and this country have been tragically numerous.

We might well ask if someone can earn almost infinite sums of money and be a Christian. Possibly. Why not "absolutely?" Because Jesus still warns, "It is easier for a camel . . ." But with God, he says, such things are possible—not certain, not easy, but not impossible either. But if someone destroys, for others as well as for themselves, everything the Kingdom of God represents, everything Jesus lived and died for, can that person be said to be his follower? Only the most radically individualistic, mechanical theory of a magical "salvation" could possibly say so.

Jesus told the story of a rich man who passed a beggar each day on his doorstep. He ignored the man and refused to care for him. The poor man died and went into the comfort of God, "into the bosom of Abraham." The rich man wound up in hell. When is enough, enough? Enough is too much if it destroys what you're trying to create, for yourself and others.

The amount of the wealth isn't the problem. Otherwise, Jesus simply would have said that riches lock the door to heaven. To the extent that money and possessions further your way; your children's way; your world's way toward human needs, human values, and human life; and to the extent those things do not destroy those values in yourself and others—they are worthwhile. Remember: "one's life does not consist in the abundance of one's possessions" (Luke 12:15).

(Not as the bumper stickers say, "He who dies with the most toys wins.") Life is measured by the gospel of Jesus Christ, the one who came "to seek and to save that which was lost"—including foolish sheep of all generations who wander off looking for just thirty percent more grass than they ate yesterday.

Second, enough is enough when life is rich, whether you are or not. Older people like to reminisce about the "good old days." (I'm not thinking of retirees and their "good old days." I'm thinking of thirty-somethings enjoying a laugh about their first apartment, executives talking about their first job, pastors talking about their church-before-last.) Invariably we describe those days as "simpler." We are always told, though, no matter what we might like, that we can't go back to those "Ozzie and Harriet" days. No, mythical days never existed in any decade, including Ozzie's. But where would you like to return? What is so appealing about those memories, even if they are selective?

In my experience, such fond stories of the past have always been connected to the very values that the gospel offers. The chance to give yourself to something that matters, time to enjoy the warmth and love of friends and family, the opportunity to appreciate and reflect upon the beauty and mystery of the creation about us—these are the riches that are often robbed from us by the frantic life forced on us by our "success."

Can we keep from getting there, this world of the rich fool? Of course. It's the one situation where "Just Say No" really works. Remember, enough is enough when life is rich, whether you are or not. We may not know how much "enough" is, but we do know when life for us is rich. And when it is, we should be very slow to "spend" our remaining time for nothing but dollars.

Can we get back from there if we've already overshot the mark in our restless acquiring, in our desperate, competitive ladder climbing? Can we find true wealth if we've already destroyed for ourselves, and perhaps for our family and others, part of the life Jesus intended? Of course. That's the message of grace in the gospel of Jesus. Turning around isn't always easy, and it's always costly. But it can be done. Forget "lifestyle." Go for life. If that means stepping back, or even stepping down, so what? People all around us are living on less money, or with less prominence, or whatever. It *can* be done, if it must be, to find your life again.

A friend of mine recently said to his son who was concerned about the expensive special education his family needed to get for him and the financial sacrifices it would cost the family: "Son, if you had a rare disease, you know we would pay for it, don't you? This is just as important to us, because it is important to your life."

When is enough, enough? Enough is enough when you don't destroy what you're trying to create; when life is rich, whether you are or not.

Notes

[1] Walter Rauschenbusch, *Dare We Be Christians?* (New York: Pilgrim Press, 1914) 46-48.

[2] Annie Dillard, *The Writing Life* (New York: Harper & Row, 1989) 17-18.

[3] Walter Brueggemann, *Finally Comes The Poet* (Minneapolis: Fortress Press, 1989) 108.

[4] Ibid., 91-98.

[5] Robert Penn Warren, *New and Selected Poems 1923-1985* (New York: Random House, 1985) 112.

Chapter 6

MEEKNESS

The Bold Shall Inherit the Freeways

Jesus taught that "the meek shall inherit the earth" (Matt 5:5, quoting Ps 37:11 [KJV]). Maybe, but they'll never get onto the freeways. Let's face it. If there is one virtue we don't want today, it's meekness. It just doesn't fit our lifestyle. Who would put "meek" as a description of themselves on their professional resume? In fact, if a prospective employer read such a description we could be sure somebody else would get the job. The term "meek" cropped up again during the recent savings and loan scandals. At Lincoln Savings and Loan, headed by Charles Keating, an in-house memo was circulated that said, "The weak, the meek, and the ignorant are always good targets."

No Meek Greeks

Arrogant scorn for the meek of the earth may seem to be a modern attitude, but it isn't. The ancient Greeks had no positive connotations for "meekness" or "humility." To be meek or humble was to be weak, servile, and insignificant. Xenophon described an insignificant river, for example, as "meek" or "humble." Demosthenes used the word to refer to the trivial power of a weak city. In the aristocratic culture of ancient Greece, the worth of a person was strictly determined by parentage. A noble mind and virtue were inherited and could not be acquired. No amount of education could change a person's status. Aristotle said that those who have grown up in poverty are totally of low character. The high-born were the masters, the lowly were the lowly, and that was that.

Slaves alone were to be meek and submissive. They had to be humble; no one else should ever humble himself or herself (although in Greek society, most "hers" were kept humble enough simply by being female). Aristotle said that a person should never contradict someone who acts humble. That attitude merely shows one to be weaker and gives the other person the advantage. In Greek society, in fact, treachery and deceit were regarded as virtues. To trick someone merely proved you were shrewder than the other person. Advantage was seized by any means possible. Even loyalty to the state was not higher than individual success.

One famous Greek general went over to the enemy when he realized Athens would fall. Later he was regarded by the Athenians as simply smart to have taken advantage of the situation. When conditions later changed, he returned to Athens and was installed triumphantly in his old post. Meekness? Servanthood? That was for slaves and failures.

But isn't that precisely the modern attitude of success? Don't we choose CEOs of companies and presidents of nations, as well as generals, by who is the "toughest"? In presidential debates, haven't the outcomes rested far more on memorable put-downs than on meaningful policy? When presidential candidate Edmund Muskie wept on the campaign trail, his bid for the presidency ended.

"The meek shall inherit the earth," Jesus said (Matt 5:5). But where? And when? Surely not in the Japanese invasion of Manchuria, nor in the slaughter of the Jews by the Nazis, nor in the Afrikaner dominance of South Africa. What was the Bible writer thinking about?

Israel understood itself as a nation of the poor, the meek, the humble. Virtually its entire history was lived in bondage to one great power or another—Egypt, Babylonia, Persia, Greece, Rome. But God had promised to bless those who were the servants of God and bring them to their promised land. God specifically chose persons who were "no people," who were not a nation, to be the people of God. The book of Judges makes it clear that the nation of Israel was made up of many tribes and nationalities. In that way no one "people" could boast in nationalistic pride that their God had accomplished their bidding. Rather, God formed this nation from many peoples so that whatever they became was entirely God's doing.

The Old Testament repeatedly shows a God who specifically chose the small and insignificant to lead. David became the hero of the people, in no small part because he was not of the kingly line. He was the twelfth son of a commoner. Again and again in Israel God chose the least likely, saved the lowly and oppressed, and overthrew the arrogant. God did that whether the oppression to his people was external or internal. The prophets warned the rich and powerful in Israel that to do injustice to the orphan and the widow was to incur the divine wrath of a just God. According to Proverbs 3:34, Yahweh will give scorn to the scorners, but God shows favor to the humble. The prophecy of Zechariah speaks of a meek and lowly messiah, a triumphant king who comes as a humble and peaceful monarch (9:9-10). He is a prince of peace, not of war, because that is God's nature.

The difference between the Hebrew and Greek concepts of meekness was profound. The Hebrews saw themselves as the children of wanderers, a powerless people in the midst of great powers. They were honored to be servants of Yahweh, the great God of all gods. The Greeks, on the other hand, stressed the primacy of the individual in a state in which power belonged to the one who could claim it. Yet the lowly born were doomed to their low station for life. So were women, who were among the weak, dominated by their husbands and kept out of sight or used as a concubine.

Democracy for the Greeks was the right of the male upper classes to make decisions. It also included their right to own slaves. They would agree with the saying frequently taught in our country as a definition of freedom: my freedom stops where another person's begins. But their interpretation of that idea was quite different from ours. If slaves and the lower classes were given more rights, the Greeks argued, the elite would have less rights. Democracy, therefore, meant their right to control others.

The gods of the Greeks were not beyond suffering a bit of humility themselves. They were susceptible to trickery, and Greek heroes frequently gained mastery of the gods through deceit. The Greeks detested the Eastern practice of prostration before gods or kings, and when Alexander the Great tried to introduce it, possibly to indicate his divine status, it met with strong resistance. These different understandings of the Greeks and Hebrews regarding the divine and of humanity caused humility to become a joke to the Greeks and a virtue to the Hebrews.

A New Humility

Meekness and humility are prominent concepts in the New Testament as well as in the Old Testament. In the birth narratives of Jesus, Mary sings of the grace of God upon "the lowliness of his servant" and of the might of God to bring down "the powerful from their thrones" and to lift up the lowly (Luke 1:48, 52). When God announced the messiah's coming, the glorious revelation of his birth was given to shepherds, the lowest of the low in Hebrew society. In fact, shepherds were so notoriously untrustworthy that they were not allowed to testify in a court of law.

Women also, whose opinions were regarded as inconsequential, could not testify in court. But in the Gospel accounts, women were the first to learn of the resurrection of Jesus and were given the assignment of telling the good news to the male apostles. So the two greatest pieces of divine news in the Christian tradition, the birth of Jesus and his resurrection, both were entrusted to the lowest and most humble in human society.

The teachings of Jesus likewise emphasized the virtues of meekness and humility. "For all who exalt themselves will be humbled, and those who humble themselves will be exalted" (Luke 14:11). This saying concludes a parable that functions both as a wisdom saying, such as those in Proverbs, and as a principle of the new kingdom of God. Just as those who rush to get the most honored seats at a wedding banquet are humiliated when they are made to move lower because someone more distinguished has arrived, so those who exalt themselves in life will be humbled before God. Conversely, those who are humble—that is, who recognize their true place as servants of God—will be exalted in the new reign of God. This same saying is repeated following the story of the proud Pharisee and the humble tax collector (Luke 18:9-14).

Jesus also taught that it is easier for a camel to go through the eye of a needle than for the rich to enter heaven (Matt 19:24). This saying shocked even his closest disciples. Who then could enter? Jesus said that it was humanly impossible, but with God all things were possible. In other words, only through humble trust in God could the rich attain heaven. Otherwise, they would place faith in their riches, and that would prove futile. We must all become humble as little children, Jesus said, or we will never see the kingdom of heaven.

Furthermore, Jesus taught that the one who would be greatest among his disciples must become the servant of all (Matt 23:11). If the greatest in the kingdom of heaven is the one who is humble like a child, then the one who would be greatest among the disciples must be the greatest in service. This message is reinforced by the fact that the Aramaic word for servant and child is the same.

Meekness

So to the disciples who were bickering over future positions of greatness in the kingdom of God, Jesus pointed to a new standard. Unlike their own culture in Israel, where questions of greatness and rank pervaded all social situations—at weddings, at meals, in questions of justice, and in all business dealings—they were to have another standard. The service of love, rather than the position of honor, was to be their goal. This surprising reversal was based on nothing less than Jesus' own model (Mark 10:43-45). Their position as servants of God carried with it the dignity of God's own authority as the one who sent them, even as Jesus, too, was sent to the world (Mark 9:36-37). Jesus taught his disciples that because God takes us seriously in our lowly state, we also must take others seriously regardless of their station in life.

On the other hand, Jesus never asked his disciples to adopt any of the visible signs of humility that characterized some pious individuals in that day (Matt 6:16-18). They were told specifically, in fact, that they were not to change their facial expression ("look dismal") or put on unusual garb to indicate their repentance or fasting. Jesus taught, as did the prophets, that true religion must be internal, of the heart, not external and for show. "Rend your hearts and not your clothing" (Joel 2:13). To the contrary, the followers of Jesus were to put oil on their heads and wash their faces, as they would for a feast (Matt 6:17).

In other words, the humility that Jesus taught does not call for gloomy faces and morbid living. It is in fact a celebration, a matter of joy. Just as God does not feel "put upon" to care for us, and as Jesus did not feel robbed to take on the form of a humble servant, Christ's disciples are not to feel burdened by servanthood. We are to remember the joy of giving. ("It is more blessed to give than to receive," Acts 20:35; a striking saying, given as a direct quotation from Jesus but not found in the Gospels.) The society of biblical times, and even ours today, usually associated "sackcloth and ashes," physical denial, or even self-flagellation with humility. But these are only outward and possibly superficial signs of sorrow or repentance. The ongoing, daily, living humility that Jesus taught is an unconscious, open acceptance of ourselves and others as children of God.

Nevertheless, when we hear the Old Testament refer to Moses as very meek or humble, "more so than anyone else on the face of the earth" (Num 12:3), it still sounds strange to us. Our ideas of meekness or humility simply don't correspond with the dramatic, insistent, sometimes angry figure of Moses of the exodus or wilderness experience. For that matter, when Jesus described himself as meek, or gentle (Matt 11:29), it is not easy to reconcile that image with his violent Sabbath disputes with the scribes and lawyers that immediately follow. And the scene in the temple courtyard in Jerusalem, when Jesus overturned the tables of the money-changers and braided a rope into a whip, seems completely contradictory. We can certainly identify personally with the temper of Moses or the anger of Jesus. But how can those images be reconciled with meekness or humility?

What Meekness Is Not

Meekness does not imply a fearful, timid existence. Nothing in either the Old Testament or New Testament view of humility implies that a "meek" person is a timid Milquetoast. If so, neither Moses nor Jesus would qualify as meek. The servanthood that takes God and people seriously requires great courage. Sometimes that courage even means boldly questioning God, as Moses did in the wilderness of Sinai and Jesus did in the garden of Gethsemane. It certainly means risking life's dangers on behalf of God's children, wherever they may be.

More than a decade ago, two Catholic sisters were on an ancient lake steamer crossing Lake Victoria, bound for the remote West Lake district of Tanzania. It was late evening, and everyone on board the decrepit old ship was hot and exhausted. The wind from the lake was cool, and almost all of the passengers had remained on the deck of the ship to catch the refreshing breezes. Most among the throng of people that had crowded on board would sleep on the decks, too, rather than sweltering restlessly in the tiny cabins.

The sisters wore no garb to identify themselves as nuns. Their clothing was rough and ordinary, and their faces were weatherbeaten from years in the intense African sun. But their voices were cheerful and enthusiastic as they talked of returning to their little clinic on the edge of nowhere. "On the other side of the Great Commission," in fact, was how missionaries in Tanzania described that distant area beyond the vast lake.

The strength and energy of those sisters, serving the children of God in a remote and comfortless place, are part of the biblical definition of meekness. Such confidence in the hand of God, even in the most desperate conditions of life, typifies all true servants of God, whether Moses in the desert, or Jesus on the cross, or two battle-worn women of mercy in the African outback, or a rabbi in a Nazi concentration camp.

At the time of Hanukkah in Bergen-Belsen, shortly before the end of the World War II, the Rabbi of Bluzhov was faced with a dilemma. All day the guards had taken prisoners at random from among the Jews for beating and death. Now darkness had come, and from their rags the prisoners had made wicks and a Hanukkah lamp. The rabbi had begun chanting the traditional blessings, but at the third blessing he hesitated. He looked about at the others for a moment, then continued: "Blessed are thou, O Lord our God, Ruler of the Universe, who has kept us alive, and has preserved us and enabled us to reach this season."

After the ceremony, one of the listeners took the rabbi aside to scold him for saying such a blessing with the dead lying even at their doors. The Rabbi of Bluzhov responded:

> When I reached the third blessing, I also hesitated and asked myself, what should I do with this blessing? I turned my head in order to ask . . . the other distinguished rabbis who were standing near me, if indeed I might recite the blessing. But just as I was turning my head, I noticed that behind me a throng was standing, a large crowd of living Jews, their faces expressing faith, devotion, and concentration as they were listening to the rite of the kindling of the Hanukkah lights. I said to myself, if God, blessed be He, has such a nation that at times like these . . . when death is looking from every corner, if despite all . . . they stand in throngs and with such devotion listening to the Hanukkah blessing . . . if, indeed, I was blessed to see such a people with so much faith and fervor, then I am under a special obligation to recite the third blessing.[1]

This is the true meekness of the people of God, those who wait like children before God and have God alone to trust for their todays and their eternities. Only true meekness can continue reciting the words of faith in the face of that kind of worldly power and evil.

Yet, even as we read the words of the rabbi, we feel our anger rising above our grief. Is it God's way to tolerate such evil, to yield docilely to such monstrous oppression of life? If that is meekness, is it not an unwitting collaborator with the imperial power of evil? Must the meek be passive?

Anger is not excluded from the person of meekness. In one Greek usage of the word, "meek" signifies a position between excessive anger and excessive angerlessness. Jesus plainly had a temper. If his explosion in the temple had been anything less than that, it never would have been recorded that way in the Gospels. A disruptive demonstration against the temple system plainly did not help the Christian cause with Jews in the first century, so we know it was no less graphic than described.

Jesus was "meek and gentle," but he certainly wasn't "mild." His outrage in the temple was directed against those who changed the worship of God into the cheating of the poor and the stranger. God's house was to be a house of prayer "for the nations" (Mark 11:17). But in the one place at the temple where all people could pray, the court of the Gentiles, a "den of robbers" was operating with the full sanction of the temple authorities. Here, true meekness demanded decisive action.

Still we have questions about "Christian anger." Why was Jesus fierce in the temple encounter, yet silent before Pilate? Why did he overturn tables at the temple and refuse to resist in the Garden of Gethsemane? What is the difference between meekness and timidity? Or between "righteous indignation" and rage?

In a later section I'll deal with anger in more detail. But for now imagine reversing Jesus' responses in the situations just described. He saw the fraud at the temple, and he was silent; he was confronted by Pilate, and he braided a whip and struck him with it. Those are examples of timidity and rage instead of meekness and moral anger.

The folks who coined the term "righteous indignation" were likely trying to excuse the anger of Jesus. But in a way, they were right. Meekness is not the absence of anger, it is anger for the right reasons. Meekness shows anger at those wrongs that make God angry. Meekness is not a doormat for the arrogant to wipe their feet. But neither is anger a whip or a sword for Christians to attack their enemies. We are advised to be "slow to anger." That's because most of our anger isn't righteous, it's self-serving. Meekness knows when to keep silent and when to overturn the tables of the exploiters of God's children.

That leads me to a third conclusion. *Meekness, such as Jesus taught and lived, has nothing to do with passive, indecisive, compliant conduct.* Essentially, true humility means acknowledging God as Lord—that is, with authority over life—and others as children of God. Jesus was proposing an alternative to the "imperial lifestyle,"[2] as Walter

Bruggemann often refers to it, the lifestyle of arrogance and pride. Such arrogance seizes power, tyrannizes the weak, and takes every advantage possible over others. Justice becomes impossible. Violence is not only tolerated but actively employed in its many forms. No contradictions to this imperial lifestyle are allowed. Only when the ruling *junta*, whatever form it takes, is acknowledged as lord and god is mere existence allowed for the weak.

Money, of course, is the engine that drives this imperial machine in every generation, just as it was in the temple under the puppet high priests of the Romans. Money also controls some Christians whose fearfulness of giving up some of their wealth blinds them to the needs of the poor or injustices to minorities. For a Christian to be led about by the nose by money is to capitulate to the true worldliness that favors the powerful and defrauds the weak. That worldliness leads to a "numbness" that gradually becomes indifferent to the life of others. The final result is the escalation of deceit, fraud, deprivation, and outright injury to the person of others. Jesus regarded this kind of pride as the primary indicator of godlessness. Such a life is a banquet of death. It feeds itself sumptuously while all else dies around it.

Another Alternative Lifestyle

So Jesus has proposed a radical alternative to the imperial lifestyle. He has offered a meaning to life called meekness. Those who are meek, as he was meek, are neither out of control with excessive anger nor paralyzed by excessive passivity. By acknowledging Jesus as our Lord and ourselves as God's servants, we cannot possibly lord it over others. Because God has taken us seriously, we take others seriously. Every fellow human being is regarded as equally worthy of respect. No questions of wealth, race, or power are allowed to influence our judgments. Because Christ humbled himself, not availing himself of power, and had compassion on even the most alienated in society, we must relate to others in the same way. We cannot take advantage of anyone, or any situation, to exploit their need or disadvantage. That is the lifestyle of meekness.

People in the "real world," of course, raise the inevitable question of practicality. To put it bluntly, does this style of life work? What about all the others who won't play by those rules? Wouldn't the powerful still use their advantage of power, the wealthy their advantage of wealth? Isn't God on the side of the army with the last reserves, as Napoleon cynically put it? What becomes of the meek then? How much earth do the meek inherit then? Enough to cover a six-foot box?

That is a fair question. Of course, such oppression was exactly what happened in the case of Jesus and in the history of many innocent groups and individuals. They were trampled under the heel of imperial tyranny. We cannot ignore reality. In spite of the worth of such a life of humility, unquestionably most of the world will never play by those rules. Jesus died under the brass-knuckled fist of the imperial lifestyle. Others have been enslaved, forced into generations of grinding poverty, or outright murdered by those who used their money and power to dominate. On a more "socially acceptable" level, the privileged have unfairly seized advantage in everything from job promotions to real estate deals to Little League baseball line-ups. Might may not make right, but it often makes the headlines.

We would be foolish to ignore the risks on the personal level from this kind of life. The meekness of Jesus brought him into dangerous confrontation with those who recognized its threat to their imperial reign. Rather than offering a sheltered, nonconfrontive life, Christlike meekness provides exactly the opposite. And it has done so again and again historically to those who have tried to live it. Meekness, seen in this light, is not a life of shrinking cowardice but of raw courage. Is it worth it? Does it change anything, this life of humility?

Look at this world. Everything good in it has been created by such an attitude, and everything evil by its opposite. The abolition of slavery, the writing of child labor laws, the end of segregation, the equal opportunity laws for minorities, the extension of care to the elderly and the very young, the bending of international swords into plowshares—all these transformations of society represent the triumph of true meekness over imperial arrogance. Take another look at those terrible tragedies in Nazi Germany, Manchuria, and South Africa. Imperial Japan and Nazi Germany paid a terrible price in destruction and death for their tyranny. South Africa was convulsed as the price of its injustice until it feared the lowly ones and listened to their prophets. Is there really any doubt that eventually everywhere on the face of God's earth the meek shall possess the land?

The courageous sacrifices of many of God's meek have made possible the advantages of freedom and justice we enjoy. The death of

Jesus at the hand of the arrogant has resulted in more powerful changes in this world than any armed revolution his disciples might have hoped to accomplish.

Jürgen Moltmann, one of the greatest modern theologians, was once a seventeen-year-old soldier in the German army. In the very last days of World War II, the fanatical Nazis in desperation forced the very young and very old into combat. With his world shattered and destroyed around him, Moltmann had no will to fight and no desire to support the Nazi cause. He surrendered in Belgium to the first British soldier he saw and was placed in a prisoner of war camp. He was hungry, dirty, and deeply depressed.

Then an American army chaplain went through the camp, handing out Bibles translated into German. Moltmann took one, although he came from an entirely secular family and was not at all religious himself. As he read of the death of Jesus and his cry of helplessness on the cross, Moltmann felt a deep companionship with God. If Jesus suffered so, Moltmann thought, as helpless as he, then perhaps God could understand and comfort him. It was not the triumphant God of a heavenly throne who spoke to him, but the suffering Christ of the cross. And as in the lives of countless others, the humble Jesus brought hope, and eventually new life, to a miserable German boy.

Another theologian, Dietrich Bonhoeffer, also suffered during World War II as a prisoner. He was a prisoner of the Nazis for his complicity in a plot on Hitler's life. Just days before the arrival of the American army, Bonhoeffer was hanged by the Gestapo. His writings from prison express many of the same feelings as Moltmann's concerning the humility of Christ and the strange, transforming power of his powerless suffering:

> God lets himself be pushed out of the world onto the cross. God is weak and powerless in the world, and that is precisely the way, the only way, in which God is with us and helps us. Matthew 8:17 makes it quite clear that Christ helps us, not by virtue of his omnipotence, but by virtue of his weakness and suffering.
>
> Here is the decisive difference between Christianity and all religions. Man's religiosity makes him look in his distress to the power of God in the world: God is the *deus ex machina* [the "god from the machine," referring to the appearance of a god at the moment of crisis in classical Greek drama]. The Bible diverts man to God's powerlessness and suffering; only the suffering God can help.[3]

The meekness of the suffering God conveyed hope and life to these Christian prisoners when easier, cheaper answers would have been meaningless. Through their sacrifices, and those of the others like them who have pointed the world toward the truth, meekness triumphs over arrogance, and humanity draws nearer the life God planned.

Nevertheless, we have to admit that this triumph of meekness remains largely a mystery to us. In our world, the team with the most points at the end of the game is the winner; "the one who dies with the most toys wins." These are rules we can understand, rules our lives have been built upon. Yet God insists on a different set of rules, where winning is sometimes losing, and losing is sometimes winning. If that were not true, God should simply use violence to rescue all victims of whatever—disease, violence, injustice—and blast all the arrogant to kingdom come. But as Jon Sobrino has written,

> That God should permit victims to suffer and die is an insurmountable scandal. In the midst of such a situation, a believer can only accept the fact that God on the cross is as impotent as the victims themselves, and then interpret such impotency as God's way of being in solidarity with those victims. The cross on which God is placed is the most eloquent proclamation that God loves the victimized of this world. On that cross God's love is impotent yet believable. And it is from that perspective that the mystery of God must be reformulated.[4]

Nonetheless, often we have been told by the church that God is "omnipotent, omniscient, and omnipresent" (and perhaps polysyllabic!). So human beings strive to be the same—powerful, infallible, limitless. Then when life crashes in, we demand that God use all those "omnis" to get us and ours out of it—and soon. Religion is held on to by many people only as the ultimate "gold card" to get whatever money and power cannot obtain otherwise.

Yet the way of power is not God's way, and God's own self becomes part of the sacrifice of meekness. Two remarkable pieces of literature perhaps explain it best. First, a strange, parabolic story by Annie Dillard:

> One bad winter in the Arctic, and not too long ago, an Algonquin woman and her baby were left alone after everyone else in their winter camp had starved. Ernest Thompson Seton tells it. The woman

walked from the camp where everyone had died, and found at a lake a cache. The cache contained one small fishhook. It was simple to rig a line, but she had no bait, and no hope of bait. The baby cried. She took a knife and cut a strip from her own thigh. She fished with the worm of her own flesh and caught a jackfish; she fed the child and herself. Of course she saved the fish gut for bait. She lived alone at the lake, on fish, until spring, when she walked out again and found people. Seton's informant had seen the scar on her thigh.[5]

Somehow the scarred God, who allowed Jesus the innocent one to know death, is better able to understand us and save us from ourselves than any "omni" God. G. A. Studdert Kennedy, a chaplain in World War I and later a brilliant theologian and preacher, expressed that conclusion in a quite different way in his dialect poem, "The Sorrow of God." An old cockney soldier struggled to make sense of the death all around him in the bloody trenches.

> The sorrows o' God must be 'ard to bear
>   If 'E really 'as Love in 'Is 'eart,
> And the 'ardest part i' the world to play
>   Must surely be God's part.
> And I wonder if that's what it really means,
>   That Figure what 'angs on the Cross.
> I remember I seed one t'other day
>   As I stood wi' the captain's 'oss. . . .
> I remember, I thinks, thinks I to mysel',
>   It's a long time since 'E died,
> Yet the world don't seen much better to-day
>   Then when 'E were crucified.
> It's allus the same, as it seems to me,
>   The weakest must go to the wall,
> And whether 'e's right, or whether 'e's wrong,
>   It don't seem to matter at all. . . .
> And they say 'E were jus the image o' God.
>   I wonder if God shed tears,
> I wonder if God can be sorrowin' still,
>   And 'as been all these years.
> I wonder if that's what it really means,
>   Not only that 'E once died,
> Not only that 'E came once to the earth

And wept and were crucified?
Not just that 'E suffered once for all
    To save us from our sins,
And then went up to 'Is throne on 'igh
    To wait till 'Is 'eaven begins.
But what if 'E came to the earth to show,
    By the paths o' pain that 'E trod,
The blistering flame of eternal shame
    That burns in the heart o' God?
O God, if that's 'ow it really is,
    Why, bless ye, I understands,
And I feels for you wi' your thorn-crowned 'ead
    And your ever pierced 'ands.
But why don't ye bust the show to bits,
    And force us to do your will?
Why ever should God be suffering so
    And man be sinning still?
Why don't ye make your voice ring out,
    And drown these cursed guns?
Why don't ye stand with an outstretched 'and,
    Out there 'twixt us and the 'Uns?
Why don't ye force us to end the war
    And fix up a lasting peace?
Why don't ye will that the world be still
    And wars for ever cease?
That's what I'd do, if I was you,
    And I had a lot o' sons
What squabbled and fought and spoilt their 'ome,
    Same as us boys and the 'Uns.
And yet, I remember, a lad o' mine,
    'E's fightin' now on the sea,
And 'e were a thorn in 'is mother's side,
    And the plague o' my life to me.
Lord, 'ow I used to swish that lad
    Till 'e fairly yelped wi' pain,
But fast as I thrashed one devil out
    Another popped in again.
And at last, when 'e grew up a strappin' lad,
    'E ups and 'e says to me,
"My will's my own and my life's my own,
    And I'm goin', Dad, to sea."

> And 'e went, for I 'adn't broke 'is will,
>   Though God know 'ow I tried,
> And 'e never set eyes on my face again
>   Till the day as 'is mother died.
> Well, maybe that's 'ow it is wi' God,
>   'Is sons 'ave got to be free;
> Their wills are their own, and their lives their own,
>   And that's 'ow it 'as to be.
> So the Father God goes sorrowing still
>   For 'Is world what 'as gone to sea,
> But 'E runs up a light on Calvary's height
>   That beckons to you and me.
> The beacon light of the sorrow of God
>   'As been shinin' down the years,
> A-flashin' its light through the darkest night
>   O' our 'uman blood and tears.[6]

"Take my yoke upon you, and learn from me," Jesus said, "for I am gentle and humble in heart, and you will find rest for your souls" (Matt 11:29). This is the promise of a new life and a new world to God's courageous meek.

Notes

[1] Yaffa Eliach, *Hasidic Tales of the Holocaust*, (New York: Avon, 1982) 14-16.

[2] Walter Bruggeman, *Finally Comes The Poet*, (Minneapolis: Fortress Press, 1989) 16.

[3] Dietrich Bonhoeffer, *Letters and Papers from Prison*, ed. Eberhard Bethge, trans. Reginald Fuller (New York: Macmillan, 1971) 360-61.

[4] Jon Sobrino, "Awaking from the Sleep of Inhumanity," *The Christian Century*, 3 April 1991, 368.

[5] Annie Dillard, *The Writing Life* (New York: Harper, 1989) 12-13.

[6] G. A. Studdert Kennedy, "The Sorrow of God," *The Unutterable Beauty* (London: Morrison and Gibb, 1927) 132-35.

CHAPTER 7

ANGER

The Cycle of Vengeance and the Circle of Love

"A man's greatest joy is to break his enemies."
—Ghengis Khan

"Love your enemies; do good to them that despitefully use you."
—Jesus of Nazareth

Esten Younger says he never drank, smoked, or used profanity even one time in his life. For anyone these days, such a claim would be unusual. But for a ninety-five-year-old man in Texas, it verges on the incredible. He did think about cursing a man once. It happened when he was sixteen and playing basketball in high school. Many of the other players in those days were men in their twenties.

"We played this team, and they had a married man guarding me," Younger said. "He was twenty-five. I started down the floor. He reached out, hit me in the throat, and knocked me to the floor." That's when Esten got provoked. "I looked at him and thought about calling him a bad name." But Esten's good Methodist heritage was too strong for that. Instead, he saw a piece of a broken desk lying beside him. So he picked it up and smashed the man over the head with it. "Knocked him out," Younger said. "And that's the only fight I ever had."[1]

There are a lot of things about that story I like. I've known a few Esten Youngers, tall and slim and straight as a flagpole, at age ninety-five looking thirty years younger and clean as a hound's tooth in the smokin'—drinking—cussin' area. Don't mess with them, though, or like that old boy in the gym found out, they'll smack you in the face with a desktop—without ever saying one bad cuss-word.

Some of us watch escapist movies to sublimate our anger. *Dirty Harry* or *Rambo* get revenge on the bad guys, love from the silicon-enhanced starlets, and admiration and envy from all the rest of us.

Hollywood loves that kind of story, because we love that kind of story. Lee Marvin goes down because Gary Cooper caught him flush on the nose with a two-by-four. What's better than the sweet satisfaction of seeing a bad guy get what's coming to him, especially from a clean-as-a-dog's-tooth good guy? Obviously, for American moviegoers, not much. *Rambo, Walking Tall, Dirty Harry,* and a thousand westerns proved that. Those "don't-get-mad-get-even" movies made Hollywood rich at the same time they made us happy. Generation after generation, their curious mixture of honor, justice, revenge and violence proves irresistible.

It's more than a casual pleasure, too, this craving for frontier justice. It's more like an appetite in the human body, a drive like hunger or thirst or sex. We need it. We're frustrated when we don't get it. It's the way things ought to be. It's right. It makes sense. And it sells.

A World of Violence

What doesn't make sense is the real world those secular myths evade. Try Esten Younger's move on a New York City playground today, or even in a rural Texas junior high gym, and see what happens. If the other guy's friends don't cripple you on the spot, you've got to worry later about his relatives. Even the mammas settle scores these days. One thing leads to another. A desktop follows a forearm, a razor follows a stilson wrench, and a pistol follows a razor. Action brings reaction, injury demands retaliation, retaliation leads to escalation: Republic of Ireland and Northern Ireland; Israel and the West Bank; Bosnians, Croats, and Serbs.

We shake our heads in amazement. Are those people crazy or what? We finish our sandwiches on the TV tray. The wife says, "Turn off the news before you get an ulcer; that stuff's depressing. Let's watch something fun. Put on that Ninja video the kids were watching." Then we listen to the local news. It begins as always with fifteen minutes of the latest, most horrific killings, rapes, and car crashes. Then we go to bed, still shaking our heads over those crazy people in Bosnia. What's the matter with this world, anyway?

Someone driving through any Southern crossroads town thirty years ago could be sure of seeing three establishments: a church, a bank, and a general store with a gas pump out front. Today the church and the bank are still there, but the gas pump is gone and the storefront has new lettering on the glass: "Karate Lessons." Every town in the South has a place to learn karate, if not some more arcane style of Oriental self-defense. It may be unAmerican to buy Japanese automobiles, but even Southern good old boys want their kids to learn Japanese self-defense tactics.

We are afraid, and why not? Our world is dizzy with violence. Internationally, nations go on making war on their own people as well as on each other. Terrorists' bombs explode in airliners over Scotland and in front of federal buildings in Oklahoma. Students demonstrate for democracy in China and get run down in the streets by government tanks. The Unabomber threatens to blow up an airliner at LAX, and transportation through Los Angeles goes into chaos. That's our world. It has become a world of assault, arson, rape, robbery, and murder; of silent killers and screaming street gangs; of high school students holding their teachers and classmates hostage. Tragically, as we seem to learn more day by day, it is also a world of child abuse and battered women. No wonder we're jittery, bordering on paranoia, and angry at the world.

Beneath this visible level of public violence in our society is another level of silent, sometimes invisible aggression. It's a level with no police or social workers, and no priests or ministers will call. This home-grown variety of violence is well-known to all of us. Getting even on the private level, revenge on a small scale, is as old as Eden.

Teenagers spread nasty rumors about someone they envy. They use a car key to scratch the side of a BMW that someone richer owns. We get back psychologically and professionally at people we work with. We blame someone else for the stolen fruit we wanted to eat. Doctors or lawyers infer that a rival is incompetent, a crook, or both. A jealous minister warns a pulpit selection committee that they wouldn't hire a fellow minister, "if you knew what I know about him." Silent violence of this sort is active in every profession, school, and neighborhood. Esten Younger, where are you when we need you?

Revenge and Retaliation

Revenge is increasingly regarded in our society as only right, the natural and even required response to hurt. Pacifism is seen merely as an excuse for cowards, not a subject for serious debate. "Do before done unto" is the primary commandment for survival in our jungle of life, and the second is like unto it: "Speak softly but carry a large-caliber weapon." And don't forget the bumper-sticker gospel: "An armed society is a polite society."

Walter Wink, however, questions the effectiveness of this "big stick" approach to violence, both morally and practically. What the New Testament refers to as "the world" (*kosmos*), he says, is that

> network of powers—political, economic, cultural, ideological—that have turned their backs on their divine vocations and idolatrously set themselves up in defiance of God.[2]

Wink calls this the "Domination System." These oppressors rely upon force and violence to dominate and exploit others. He argues, however, that those who use the methodology of this system are invariably damaged by it and stand in danger of becoming the very thing they oppose. Jesus said to Pilate,

> My kingdom is not from this world. If my kingdom were from this world, my followers would be fighting to keep me from being handed over to the Jews. But as it is, my kingdom is not from here. (John 18:36)

In other words, since his way of life is not the world's (*kosmos*) way of life, his disciples are not to use the world's methods of violence—not even to protect righteousness. Jesus laid down his life without resistance to deliver humanity from this evil order of violence. Only the willingness of his disciples to take up their crosses of injustice in daily life, he said, rather than a sword, can enact his way in the world.

Yet, like Simon in the garden, our fears betray us. Wink wrote:

> Like so many of us who are willing to espouse nonviolence only as long as it is successful, Peter is prepared in the garden for the worst; he draws his sword and chops off the ear of the high priest's servant. I have never seen a commentary on the ineffectiveness of Peter's wild display of swordsmanship, but it deserves comment. After all, one of the delusions of the Domination System is that one is safer from attack when armed. . . . this same delusion keeps our country heavily supplied with guns, despite statistics that indicate that the majority of storeowners who pull a gun in self-defense are shot; that homicides are three times more likely in households where guns are present than in households where they are not; that three-fourths of the victims of guns in homes are killed not by intruders but by a spouse, family member, or friend.[3]

Granted, it's not easy for Christians to be consistent on the subject of retaliation. The *Orlando Sentinel* recently polled its readers on suggestions for students who are regularly confronted with abuse from violent bullies at school. In the November 17, 1994 issue, Ron Henkel, a Navy man home on leave, wrote these words:

> Jesus basically says, "Hey, turn the other cheek." That's got to be just as tough as joining a gang. . . . I believe in what Jesus says. Why not take the nonviolent approach? That's the way to show what kind of man he is.

We can't blame Henkel for failing to notice the ironic inconsistency of his position. He advocates a "nonviolent approach" to a schoolchild struck by a bully, while he works for a Navy prepared to launch retaliatory sub missiles at a moment's notice. Yet he is sincerely convinced that he "believes in what Jesus says." But in which position? In not retaliating with violence, or in eliminating one's enemies?

Are we all not just as confused? Get struck, strike back, personally or nationally. On one level, we know that kind of thinking is wrong. On another level, it makes sense to us. We are afraid, so we arm ourselves. Shoot first, find out who it is later. Kill those who kill before they can kill again. "An eye for an eye," that's justice. Let the punishment fit the crime. It's only fair. After all, isn't that exactly what Leviticus 24:19-20 says in gruesome detail in the *Lex Taliones,* the law of retaliation?

Most of us have only heard "an eye for an eye" from the law. Here's the rest of it:

> Anyone who kills a human being shall be put to death. Anyone who kills an animal shall make restitution for it, life for life. Anyone who maims another shall suffer the same injury in return: fracture for fracture, eye for eye, tooth for tooth; the injury inflicted is the injury to be suffered. (Lev 24:17-20)

Obviously we don't obey that law literally today, even in those states that have the death penalty. Nevertheless, many Christians argue for the death penalty from this scripture. They deny that their belief comes from revenge; they insist that it comes from obeying the simple, literal words of the Bible. But if that is so, why do we not extract the eyes of those who blind others, or knock out a tooth from a junior high boy who knocks out our boy's tooth?

The *Lex Taliones* was given in the context of a speech of Moses. He was attempting to settle the case of an Israelite woman's son who had blasphemed the Name (of God) in a curse. Moses' reply to her situation comes just one verse before the *Lex Taliones*. He said that anyone who blasphemes the Name shall be put to death. Now if that law were pursued as religiously as the fervor for the death penalty in the United States, there might not be enough people left to carry out the sentence. Strange, isn't it, how legalistic we are about carrying out ancient Hebrew death sentences when we have been wronged, but how indifferent we are about carrying out the same sentence when God has been offended?

Why are we not equally literalistic about Jesus' complete reversal of the *Lex Taliones* in Matthew 5:38-39? "You have heard that it was said, 'an eye for an eye' . . . But I say to you, Do not resist [literally, with armed force, *anthestemi*] an evildoer." Revenge by retaliation, measure for measure, is simply regarded by most of us as logical and appropriate. And belief in the laws of Scripture is obviously not necessary to arrive at that conclusion, since at least as many non-Bible-believers as Bible-believers hold that position.

To be sure, an "eye-for-an-eye" law is an improvement over the unharnessed exercise of rage, an "eye-for-an-insult, a-set-of-front-teeth-for-your-dog-in-my-flowerbed." In the book of Genesis, Lamech illustrates this kind of limitless blood revenge: "I have killed a man for wounding me, a young man for striking me" (4:23-24). Lamech's macho kind still hang out in countless bars, looking for trouble, and strike down other drivers in freeway shootings for imagined insults. An "eye for an eye," even an electric chair for a murder, is certainly an improvement over limitless, lawless revenge.

But is appropriate retaliation the final law for humanity? If so, why did Jesus say these words in the same context quoted previously? "You have heard that it was said, 'an eye for an eye'. . . . But I say to you, Love your enemies and pray for those who persecute you" (Matt 5:38-44). Some response other than revenge must be expected of a Christian, even some response other than retaliation in equal measure.

Punishment and Justice

What are we to do, then, with our anger? Our justifiable outrage at murders and violations of human rights, from children by their parents to whole ethnic groups exterminated by those who hate them? Are we to be indifferent to injustice, passive at crimes against persons?

Are Christians to undergo some kind of moral prefrontal lobotomy so that our emotions are severed from reality?

How then could we explain the anger of Jesus at the exploitation of humble pilgrims in the temple court, his so-called "cleansing of the temple"? Remember that he even braided a rope whip and chased the money-changers out of the temple precincts. (I was always told that Jesus had "righteous indignation"; we have anger. But righteous indignation is merely anger spelled with twenty letters.)

There is no easy answer to the question of punishment and justice. Well-intended Christians have wrestled seriously with this problem from the first century to the twenty-first. Some of them believe in capital punishment; others believe in no death penalty. Some believe in a "just war" theory; others believe in absolute pacifism. All believe they have biblical, if not gospel, warrant for their views.

Little wonder the church has sounded various notes on the subject. Parts of the church have always refused violence, regarded war as evil, and shunned anger. The Anabaptists, the early Methodists, the Quakers, the Seventh-Day Adventists, and others suffered considerably, sometimes even died, for their pacifistic views. On the other hand, at times the church has not only participated in wars but sponsored them. (These, of course, were "holy" wars.) The Crusaders swallowed more war than they could digest when they attacked the "infidel" to "liberate" Palestine. Crazy hermits, pompous knights, and even small children trooped away to fight in God's name, or something like that. When the whole affair was over and the few who lived limped home, everybody was more than willing to stay in their own backyards—at least for the time being.

Smaller vendettas, but more savage yet, were carried out in the Spanish Inquisition against Jews and other deviants from the holy Catholic faith. For the sake of the Protestant Reformation, Martin Luther approved the drowning of Anabaptists, both men and women, and John Calvin had Michael Servetus burned at the stake. Protestant zealots in Switzerland destroyed Catholic churches and anyone who stood in their way. Huguenots (French Protestants) were slaughtered in the streets of Paris for defying Catholic authority—and so on and so on, you know the story. It's long and not very pretty.

Wars, Pacificism, and American Anger

As usual, the issue gets entangled in questions of patriotism, which is the optimistic word for nationalism. Early Baptists in this country were strongly pacifistic, as well such a persecuted minority might be. But they rallied strongly behind the American Revolution, fighting in it and furnishing chaplains for it. The Methodists refused to do so. As a result, Baptists for the first time became regarded as part of the American mainstream and their popularity rose considerably. Methodists, on the other hand, got a black eye it took them awhile to get over. But they learned their lesson. Never doubt that positive reinforcement from society works, or that painful rejection doesn't cause the stoutest believers to rethink their doctrines—particularly where killing enemies is concerned.

But the costliest war in American history was yet to come. This time around, almost everybody was happy to jump in. The Civil War eclipsed every other war, before and since, in the number of Americans dead. Before the fratricide ended, 600,000 of the finest of America's citizens lay dead. The toll of that hatred and loss to this nation is incalculable. Slaves were freed, but racism exploded.

If it is true that you have to be taught to hate, the Civil War was the perfect school. Southerners and Northerners, "Rebs" and "Yanks," struggled even to exist in the same nation. At least part of the gunslinger attitude of the South is as much due to Civil War hangover as to the often-cited "frontier spirit" of the region. A bellicose spirit arose from that war and entered the bloodstream of a people not noted for much gentle forbearance in the first place. Preachers North and South had endorsed a war of brother against brother. How could they ever again preach turning the other cheek or loving an enemy?

Nevertheless, after the next war, World War I, many denominations in America were shocked and exhausted by its enormous toll. Never before had so many Americans died on foreign soil. A spirit of isolationism swept the nation. The League of Nations idea was too grand and idealistic for a battered and still provincial United States. The failure of the League came as a self-fulfilling prophesy when the U.S. gave it little credence or support.

Pacifism rode the waves of prosperity that washed over the nation following World War I. Much of the church imagined that the "war to end all wars" had succeeded. It was impossible for the church to see that its blithe optimism was anchored in temporary prosperity, and that its pacifism was bolstered by a nationalistic isolationism. The giddy Twenties roared on.

Then Adolph Hitler banged his fist on the table, and the party abruptly ended. Harry Emerson Fosdick, then the most noted preacher of the American pulpit, announced that his utopian visions and those of others like him had proved wrong. In a striking sermon, "The Modern World's Rediscovery of Sin" (1939), he declared that humankind had not achieved perfection, nor was it approaching it. Rather, the brutalities of the Nazis had proved that culture and education were no remedy for the evil within human nature. Reinhold Niebuhr similarly renounced his former absolute pacifism and argued that no such position was possible for a Christian. At best, one could hold only to a limited pacifism. "Just war" theories gained increasing acceptance as the "good war" against the Axis powers came to a triumphant conclusion.

The American church was virtually unanimous in its open and enthusiastic support of the Second World War. But in the remaining years of the century, only the relatively painless thumping of the ineffective army of Saddam Hussein would ever make the American nation feel so good again about war.

Vietnam was another story. Tedious, costly, and threatening to national identity and unity, that war almost turned the country back toward isolationism if not pacifism. The church and Christians were deeply divided over the morality of that war and its human devastation. Many soldiers were embittered by the lack of national support for the war, while others returned home disillusioned by the endless, mindless devastation. The nation itself soon felt also the bitter effects of the addictions, disease, and loss of ideals that invariably accompany such dehumanizing wars. Indeed, American foreign policy had to acknowledge that it would be a long while before the nation ever again would approve sending its sons and daughters to war. Robert MacNamara's recent *apologia pro vita sua*—"we knew it was wrong at the time"—did nothing to help the situation.

Nonetheless, the humiliation and loss of self-esteem bred by the ending of the Vietnam war only increased the deep-seated anger in the American psyche. If unrequited love produces hell's fury, unfulfilled revenge must produce the devil himself. The residual anger from the frustration over Vietnam still marks and divides us, politically, racially, and spiritually.

As we now face another century, one that begins in anger and will doubtless have its own wars, what must a Christian do about anger? Can we ignore it, subliminate it, repress it? Is it possible to direct or redirect it? If so, what are its uses, its limits? Is retaliation ever justified? Should an individual retaliate? Should the state? Is participation in war ever a Christian option? What did Jesus intend for his disciples?

The Angry World of Jesus and His Response

The world of Jesus knew at least as much about anger as our own. Rome ruled Israel at the point of a sword. Hundreds, possibly thousands of Jews had been brutally murdered, many of them crucified, by Roman authorities. Taxes were outrageous, enough so to make us ashamed about our present-day complaints about taxes. Religious offices were bought and sold. Graeco-Roman culture with its spectacles, games, and plays threatened to swallow the last remnants of the Jewish way of life. The Greek language was heard everywhere in Hebrew streets, and rabbis were accused of being more adept at hurling the javelin than interpreting the Law. Young people no longer wanted to wear their traditional clothing; many wore instead the Greek hats and robes. A deep, smoldering anger glowed red-hot just beneath the surface of Jewish docility before their Roman masters.

The common people Jesus walked with, the Jewish peasants, knew plenty about anger. They bore the brunt of the taxes, both civil and religious, the labor conscriptions, the brutalities of Roman soldiers far from home in a land they despised. But they had no power and little influence. Democracies did not exist, least of all in Israel. No one sought or heard the opinions of the peasants.

What Jesus said to his followers had little chance of going further then their own homes and clans. He prescribed no global solutions to these peasants struggling to survive at the bottom of the social and economic barrel. If he had, it would have been a cruel and pointless exercise. But what he did say had the power to change them, and through them to change their children and their children's children. And someday, somehow, they would translate those teachings into plans and policies that transformed much of Western society. In this way, through his life and death, Jesus indeed brought in "the Day of the Lord" and the reign of God, both with its justice and its joy.

When we review Christ's words about anger, violence, and retaliation, we ask ourselves what they should mean for our own time, in our own lives. At the beginning, let's remind ourselves of a few facts. (1) Jesus lived as a Palestinian peasant and taught his truth to Palestinian peasants. (2) Jesus lived in a world very much like ours in some regards and completely different in others. (3) Jesus did not in any way offer a program for national jurisprudence, much less international policy. (4) Jesus also was not interested in prescribing a plan for inner harmony, personal psychological adjustment, or conflict management in home or office. (5) Jesus was focused entirely upon bringing about the will of God on earth, which he called the kingdom of God or the reign of God. He did not deviate from that purpose with reference to anger, whether talking about it or displaying it.

Now, as then, the words of Jesus about anger and retaliation are words to individuals, but they reach through individuals to their larger world. They cannot remain on the purely personal level. They cannot simply be interiorized, held so close that only our inner being hears them. These teachings are not scriptures for mere inner adjustment, for a daily moment of tranquility, a kind of religious attitude-adjustment hour, Jewish Zen for harried office workers. Such psychological nuances were trivialities upon which Jesus did not theorize.

He taught and lived the revolutionary life of the radically transforming and soon-coming kingdom of God. He had no interest in preaching our kind of increasingly-popular televised sermons: "Four Steps to a New You" or "How to Be Happy in the Lord." Nor did he advocate a withdrawal from the world. He did not urge his disciples to flee into the cloister of the monk or into The Church That Has Everything So You Won't Touch the Outside, from education to sports to entertainment. To the contrary, the words of Jesus dare us to risk rejection and hostility by refusing to accept easy answers. His gospel dares us to translate his words into policies that interpret God's will for our larger world of business, politics, and human relations.

On the other hand, none of the sayings or actions of Jesus can be used as a literal prescription for every situation. He himself reacted differently in different situations. For example, Jesus plainly did not turn the other cheek to the money-changers in the temple. Yet, in the garden, he told Simon to put away his sword, and he refused to order his followers to fight because his kingdom was "not of this world."

In the first case, the incident in the temple courtyard, Jesus made a whip in a threatening fashion; whether he used it on anyone is open to speculation. In the second case, Jesus rebuked the use of a weapon by his disciples who intended to defend him in order to protect the possibility of the kingdom of God; that is, with Jesus as a leader who could inaugurate an earthly kingdom. In another incident, he refused to allow the stoning of the woman taken in adultery. At the same time he personally repudiated the Mosaic law that plainly and literally ordered the death of an adulterous woman. In its place he posited a new law: only those without sins of their own should exercise the death penalty.

Any of these incidents, and more, could be used as warrants for specific, legalistic rules for Christian conduct or laws for secular government. Some have been used that way. The Puritans almost ruined the New England colonies with their legalism. Various Christian groups today still use different sayings or events in the Bible involving violence as absolute foundational texts for their beliefs. No sector of the Christian church, Catholic or Protestant, conservative or liberal, has a corner on this practice. We are all desperate to know exactly what we should believe, preach, and do in this complicated and critical area of life. So we yank out any text that seems to us unequivocal and wave it like a sign at others who, in turn, stand on the other side of the theological street, waving their signs at us and chanting verses from the same Bible we are quoting to them.

What is going on here? If interpreted literally, obviously any one of these texts could contradict another. How have most of us managed to overlook those other words of Jesus, the ones those other people quote? How have we come to such absolute conclusions about "our" text, when somewhere some text gives another picture?

Without knowing it, we may have formed our opinions from the conventional wisdom of our culture. We may be using a biblical text merely as an excuse to legitimize our prior conclusions. Only a broad reading of scripture and a careful attendance to its setting in the time of Jesus can point us toward the reign of God. Otherwise, in the question of anger as in others, we carve a statue of Jesus in the image of our contemporary culture. And in every such case, the face of that icon more closely resembles the face of its carver than the face of Jesus. How often does that happen? Wherever blood issues, heart-pounding issues—life, death, me, mine—are concerned, we all lean mightily into the fresh wind of the gospel as we try to make our own truth the gospel's truth.

How can we know when our conclusions are that of the prevailing culture rather than that of the gospel? No one can know for certain that they hold God's position except God. But we can strongly suspect that we don't hold God's position when the gospel always seems to say what we already believe. In other words, when God is always on your side—when God never contradicts your personal interests—you've got more than a hint that your personal gospel was written by yourself or others like you. What is an individual to do, then, with these questions of anger or retaliation? What is the state to do?

The church has lost one of the keys to life, I believe, both personal and corporate, when it has ignored the larger gospel on violence for an easy proof-text agreement with the popular majority. It is easy enough, in a conservative era such as the 1950s or the 1990s, to hold flag-waving rallies on the Fourth of July, lead cheers for "my country, right or wrong," and advocate the death penalty and the guns-unlimited policies of the N.R.A. On the other hand, it is also easy enough in liberal eras to advocate sanctified passivity in the face of aggressive evil and wistfully hope for the eventual betterment of the human race. We will never be able to spell out God's final will in these matters in specific, legislative detail, not in this era or any other. But I believe we can point to three larger truths from the life of Jesus that redirect us toward this lost key to life.

First, Jesus plainly believed in the judgment of God on sin in the world. He was eminently realistic about the human capacity for evil. Unlike some myopic liberals, he was not oblivious to the tragic realities of life, to the crimes and cruelties of rich and poor alike. He also preached that God would not ignore the indifference of those who pass by the hungry, the sick, the naked, and those in prison (Matt 25); those so-called righteous would be turned down the goat-path at the day of judgment. "Publicans and prostitutes" would enter the kingdom ahead of them. Jesus saw the truth about such hypocrites, as the prophet Jeremiah before him:

> Your iniquities have turned these away, and your sins have kept good from you. For wicked men are found among my people; they lurk like fowlers lying in wait. They set a trap; they catch men. Like a basket full of birds, their houses are full of treachery; therefore

they have become great and rich, they have grown fat and sleek. They know no bounds in deeds of wickedness; they judge not with justice the cause of the fatherless, to make it prosper, and they do not defend the rights of the needy. (5:25-28)

Walter Bruggemann says that the prophets speak "powerfully, redundantly, and without apology" about this anger of God against wickedness. "Heaven is genuinely offended by our distorted ways of living."[4] The wrath of God is real because God takes us and sin seriously. Humankind can do great hurt, serious wrong. We've proved that true in every age and nation. God cannot and does not ignore injustice. Nonetheless, God's wrath cannot be reduced to mere mechanical retribution. The one offended is the one who loves us as children, the one who has given us "unspeakable gifts." God, as our parent, is deeply wounded by our wickedness to one another:

> Because of such gifts abused, prophetic rage bespeaks the hurt that our waywardness on earth evokes in heaven. Judgment that is not understood as a form of unendurable hurt misses the point of the biblical drama.[5]

Second, the life of Christ also testifies plainly to the amazing mercy of God toward sinful humanity. If unreconstructed liberals are likely to err on the side of minimizing the seriousness of human sin, vengeful conservatives are likely to err on the side of minimizing God's grace. Extermination of the life of a murderer might well be justified on an "equal judgment" basis, a life for a life—our natural emotions tell us that—but is it God's will?

Should a Christian not factor into this equation the long-suffering nature of God toward us? Could it be that we are like those persons raising stones to cast at the woman taken in adultery, when we ourselves are also sinners and unworthy to live in God's presence? Jesus said to her, "Go, and sin no more." Should we, on the other hand, say to society's criminals, "Go to hell, you won't get a chance to sin again"? Is that our gospel? Should we abruptly terminate all options for another human being?

As individuals, we do not allow ourselves to exercise that sentence against criminals. To do so is itself a crime. But collectively as a state, we may do so. Why the difference? Granted, individual judgment is more likely to be in error. But once the state has decided the case, the result is the same. Equal punishment (more or less) is meted out for the crime—assuming the right person is being terminated—a life for a life. As citizens of the state, is not our hand also on the death switch?

Bob Ray Sanders, columnist for the *Fort Worth Star-Telegram,* wrote:

> This state (that means you, me, and our ancestors) has officially killed 464 people, more than any mass murderer in the country. No, I haven't forgotten about the victims who were viciously murdered. If killing their killers would bring them back, I'd be in favor of the death penalty. But it doesn't work that way.
>
> I could talk about the dual system of justice and how the death penalty has been administered with an emphasis on the race and social status of the victim, but I won't. I could even talk about those executed who were later proved to be innocent, but I won't.
>
> All I want to say is that the 10 people listed above [executed in 1995 in Texas] and the 454 others who went before them were human beings. And although the state has the right to mete out justice to individuals who have committed a crime, no state (just as no individual) should have the right to take a person's life.

A character in an Anton Chekov short story put it best when, arguing against the death penalty, he said: "The state is not God. It has no right to take away that which it cannot give back, if it should so desire."[6] In any case, whether or not justice is satisfied by the execution, the public is. But is God?

Christians will likely go on disagreeing over capital punishment. Life imprisonment for capital offenses, with or without parole, is costly, unpredictable, and therefore potentially dangerous. But capital punishment is even more costly, and its effects on us and our children are also unpredictable and dangerous. We do not have a specific writ from God on the subject of capital punishment, contrary to the belief of practically everyone who has ever opened a Bible. What we do have in the Bible is knowledge of God's wrath against evildoers, the evidence of God's long-suffering patience toward humankind, and the testimony of the life of Jesus to both. It is my conviction (which, I might add, I came to rather late in life) that the clear weight of Jesus' life favors forbearance over vengeance, love over hate—even for the worst offender—and life over death.

Third, we know from the life of Jesus that reconciliation is the heart of his message. The reign of God, as Jesus saw it, was all about reconciliation between God and God's children, and God's children with one another. Reconciliation with God makes reconciliation with each other possible. The parables of the Prodigal, the Good Samaritan, and countless sayings and experiences in the life of Jesus make the same point. The followers of Jesus are not to go about excluding others, judging, getting even, or striking back at others. They are to accept their worth as God's children, and in the new-found joy of that discovery they are to embrace the world of the excluded, the unaccepted, even the unclean and the unworthy. His followers are to do the ultimately unthinkable: love their enemies (Luke 6:27).

To know these three truths—that God takes seriously sin, grace and forgiveness, and reconciliation seriously, each of these attested to through the costly life and death of Jesus—God somehow believed was enough to give us the keys to our anger and natural desire for vengeance. Only as we forgive one another in the grace-filled, inclusive community of Jesus can we lay the only sure foundation for ending violence on this earth.

Bruggemann summed up these truths in this way:

> It is the hope and promise of the gospel that the community of Jesus could practice a more faithful, life-giving righteousness. In the catalogue for this mandate, Jesus asserts that anger with a brother or sister makes one subject to judgment: "So if you are offering your gift at the altar, and then remember that your brother has something against you, leave your gift before the altar and go, first be reconciled to your brother and then come and offer your gift."
>
> The new righteousness offered in the gospel occurs in a world where people like us are angry enough to kill. People who are angry enough to kill do come to church, do approach God, do bring an offering. Jesus asserts that the making of reparations precedes offerings to God. Reconciliation with one's neighbor is the prerequisite for communion with God. . . . So go to your brother, your sister, the ones you have wronged. That reconciliation is a human act, done before approaching the throne.[7]

We cannot overcome the passion of anger until we can oppose it with the passion of love. As Brueggemann said, "only a passion can overcome a passion."[8] As the children of God, we must become passionate peacemakers. Jesus said, "Blessed are the peacemakers, for they shall be called children of God." (Matt 5:9) McLeod Bryan expanded on the concept of peacemakers with this version of the beatitudes:

> Blessed are the peacemakers, for nobody else would try to overcome the odds but children of God.
> Blessed are the peacemakers, for only the divine offspring have the power to overcome.
> Blessed are the peacemakers, for with the unanimous evidence to the contrary, they still believe peace can be accomplished.
> Blessed are the peacemakers, for anyone who dares attempt what the peacemaker dares is bound to be blessed.
> Blessed are the peacemakers, for the very first perfect child of God was a peacemaker.
> Blessed are the peacemakers, for they are creating the world a second time, setting it right-side-up as God originally intended it.
> Blessed are the peacemakers, for only those empowered by God would be foolish enough to undertake such an assignment.
> Blessed are the peacemakers, for they know that they may be killed in the process of making peace.
> Blessed are the peacemakers, for they know that they will never see the peaceful era which they have given their lives for.
> Blessed are the peacemakers, for they have the last word because even the warriors and the executioners carry out their duties in the name of peace.
> Blessed are the peacemakers, for God has confirmed the final victory of peace.[9]

Christians must pass from the passion of anger to the passion of love, from the never-ending cycle of vengeance to the all-embracing circle of reconciliation. It is not in us, of ourselves, the grace to do that. But in the community of Jesus, as we consider how God is "longsuffering toward us, not willing that any should perish" (2 Pet 3:9), we can be moved from "an eye for an eye" to "love your enemies." Then, and only then, can we hold in our hands the key to the anger of the world.

Listen once more to these words of Jesus from the Sermon on the Mount:

> But I say to you that listen, Love your enemies, do good to those who hate you, bless those who curse you, pray for those who abuse you. If anyone strikes you on the cheek, offer the other also; and from anyone who takes away your coat do not withhold even your shirt. Give to everyone who begs from you; and if anyone takes

away your goods, do not ask for them again. Do to others as you would have them do to you.

If you love those who love you, what credit is that to you? For even sinners love those who love them. If you do good to those who do good to you, what credit is that to you? For even sinners do the same. If you lend to those from whom you hope to receive, what credit is that to you? Even sinners lend to sinners, to receive as much again. But love your enemies, do good, and lend expecting nothing in return. Your reward will be great, and you will be children of the Most High; for he is kind to the ungrateful and the wicked. Be merciful, just as your Father is merciful.

Do not judge, and you will not be judged; do not condemn, and you will not be condemned. Forgive, and you will be forgiven; give, and it will be given to you. A good measure, pressed down, shaken together, running over, will be put into your lap; for the measure you give will be the measure you get back. (Luke 6:27-38)

Notes

[1] John McConal, "Texas," *Fort Worth Star-Telegram*, 10 Feb 1994, 22.

[2] Walter Wink, "The Other World is Here," *The Christian Century*, 27 April 1994, 443.

[3] Ibid.

[4] Walter Bruggemann, *Finally Comes The Poet* (Minneapolis: Fortress Press, 1989) 18, 20.

[5] Ibid., 20.

[6] Bob Ray Sanders, *Fort Worth Star-Telegram*, "Death Penalty Turns All of Us into Murderers," 11 June 1995, 27A.

[7] Bruggemann, 33-34.

[8] Walter Bruggemann, *Prophetic Imagination* (Philadelphia: Fortress Press, 1978) 91.

[9] McLeod Bryan, "Against The Odds," *Baptist Peacemaker*, 1987.

CHAPTER 8

CONTENTMENT

Burnout and the Thirty-Percent Solution

In these last days of the twentieth century, we can hear discontent from every quarter of life. We are not content with our jobs, incomes, families, relationships, or society. Most of all, we are not content with ourselves. But we want to be content. We have only one small problem. We don't know what contentment is. It isn't easy to find something when you don't know what it is to begin with.

Contentment, or a Reasonable Facsimile Thereof
When most of us think of contentment, we picture an old man and woman in rocking chairs on the porch of a retirement cabin in the mountains. Old Spot lies by the couple's side in a patch of sunlight, rhythmically thumping his tail. A cat plays with a ball of yarn the woman is using in her knitting. Meanwhile, the old man is opening an envelope from Merrill Lynch that reports his $900,000 in treasury bills is doing well. They look at each other and smile. A brokerage house logo follows. That's contentment, American style.

Of course, along the way toward our cabin in the mountains we struggle to find something that will make us content until we get there. A new car always helps. In 1994 Americans bought over 20 million automobiles and pickups. That cost us a mere 150 billion dollars. The Japanese were second in the world to us in the number of automobiles purchased, and they bought half as many. We have 36,683 shopping malls in the U.S., give or take a few thousand. We spend plenty of money there, too. Recent retail sales in the U.S. for one year totaled approximately 2 billion dollars. Our priorities are straight, for sure. We spend nearly 6 billion dollars annually on lawn care alone—and we still have mole crickets, dandelions, and chinch bugs.

Naturally, we don't pay cash for all of those things. We Americans have an average of nine credit cards apiece. Do we use them? A lot? In spite of unconscionable interest rates? We must. We are $225.4 billion in debt. And still we aren't content.

One of the most depressing statistics I have ever read was in a survey that asked Americans how much more money they would need to be content, reasonably speaking. Across the board, people said they needed thirty percent more than their present income. If they could just earn thirty percent more, they would be content. Reasonable enough. What's so depressing about that? The problem is, that answer held true regardless of the amount they were earning. For example, people earning $10,000 said they needed thirty percent more to be content; people earning a million dollars a year still said they needed thirty percent more to be content. *In other words, enough money to be contented is exactly thirty percent more than we will ever earn in our lifetime—regardless of how much we earn.*

But earning money and spending it is not the only way Americans try to become content. We also think we will be more content if we change the way we look. Last year there were 11,000 beauty contests in America. Even though that's a world record, it still means that only 11,000 of us were winners. So the rest of us try to get there one way or the other. At any one time, at least 50 million adults are on a diet in this country, even though 70 to 100 percent of their loss is promptly gained back. (We also eat 16 million hamburgers a day—for fast-food contentment—which is part of the reason we're always dieting.) For the crowning touch, literally, to our looks, we spend a billion dollars a year on hair spray alone. (One comedian, needling the South about its fondness for sprayed hair, guessed that the ozone layer above Montgomery, Alabama, must be dissolved altogether.)

We are dissatisfied, for sure. We want more money. We want less weight. We want a new toy. We want something else all the time, but that something else keeps changing. We have high turnover in our jobs. We have become nomads. We move more from city to city, from house to house, than any other people on earth. And that leads to something else we want: stability. Let's face it. We just want.

Contentment and Burnout

In our search for contentment, we burn out. I have a file folder bulging with articles about people who have suffered burnout. (I started to quote a few of them. But they were so uniformly depressing, I burned out.) These are not people who didn't do things "right"; they are people who did everything right, according to our modern business-consumer culture, and who got most of the things they wanted. Then they burned out. They are mostly young adults, too, both men and women. Still, they are the lucky ones. The unlucky ones simply committed suicide.

Suicide is a national calamity in America and perhaps the most accurate indicator of a society's lack of contentment. There are now three times as many suicides in this country as there were thirty years ago. The suicide rate is high among the elderly, especially males, but it is even higher among teenagers. The peak years for suicide and depression come between the ages of fifteen and nineteen. Depression is three to four times greater in that age span than among the middle-aged, which has always been regarded as the most vulnerable period of life for depression. Every college in America is busy counseling students who are on the verge of suicide. High school counselors are kept equally busy, and the problem persists even into the elementary grades.

We might expect suicide to be more prevalent among the economically disadvantaged or in underdeveloped countries. But that is not so; to the contrary. Rich Western nations such as Sweden, Switzerland, and the United States have the highest suicide rates on earth. In fact, as disadvantaged groups climb the socio-economic ladder, their suicide rates increase. Why? Part of the reason is the increase in their expectations and the ever-lengthening distance to contentment.

For example, many people who grew up in small towns or on rural farms during the depression of the 1920s and 1930s recall those years with fondness. Granting the distortion of nostalgia and a certain romanticizing of past experience, we can still learn something from their observations. "We were poor, but didn't know it," is a phrase said often and fondly in the South and elsewhere. Those who went through the Great Depression show pride at having endured poverty and gotten through to the other side with a certain contentment in spite of it.

At least a couple of things can be noted at this point. First, the saying "we were poor, but didn't know it" explains whatever contentment they had. It is quite possible to find some contentment when your status is not below that of everyone else you know. Suicide in prosperous nations can be explained on the same basis. High suicide rates in Switzerland? In that picture-book country? Of course: when everything is supposed to be the best where you live and your life isn't happy, for whatever reason, where do you go? What do you do? The problem of suicide inevitably increases where the promises of life are unfulfilled. More suicides occur at Christmas and holiday periods for the same reason. When everyone else is happy and content, or you think they are, your sense of loneliness or discontent can be overwhelming.

Second, no one today should use such Depression-era memories to feel superior to current disadvantaged groups who are discontented. The experiences simply are not comparable. Most of the people who reflect positively on their "hard times," back whenever, nevertheless had personal resources not available to most disadvantaged persons today. Simply being white, or from families that had always achieved, gave advantages not usually recognized. Furthermore, the Depression struck families without favor, rich and poor, black and white. Today serious questions of inequality or injustice are involved with the majority of America's disadvantaged.

The lesson is plain. Contentment, or the lack of it, may not have as much to do with how many objects we possess as with our sense that others have things we don't have. In a Depression-era town, for example, the banker's kids may have had no more than the school janitor's kids (or less, if the janitor kept his job while the bank and banker went under). Then no one in town felt economically inferior or superior, and satisfaction in life had to be found on another basis. Relationships became more important as common problems formed a common bond of need between people.

When we are aware of vast differences between our standard of living and that of the wealthy, we can easily attribute our discontent to a lack of possessions. Of course, the real jolt comes when we eventually accumulate wealth and possessions but are no more contented than before. At that point disillusionment, burnout, depression, and even suicide may follow. You don't need to read the newspapers very long to realize that prosperous America suffers from all of those problems, and more.

First-Century Frustration

Our modern American doesn't sound like a very happy world. But our problems are neither novel nor modern. The world of Jesus was much like ours. His world in the first century was a world of chaos—political, economic, and social. Likely none of us, not even the Great Depression survivors, have ever lived in such economic and social calamity as the daily experience of the world of Jesus. The average lifespan in his time was forty years or less. Rome ruled the Israelites with an iron fist. Society was sharply divided between the haves and have-nots, and the have-nots were in the vast majority. Puppet rulers such as the Herods doled out favors to their friends and used the power of Rome to subjugate everyone else. The Jewish aristocracy and peasants were bitterly divided. The lower priesthood despised the upper priesthood. Since the ruling priestly class was made up of the aristocracy, the common people were also deeply suspicious of the religious hierarchy.

Such a situation never could have been imagined in the old days of the Hebrews, who were all "Depression-era" survivors of Egyptian captivity. But the old days were gone. And though they didn't know it, they were gone forever. Palestine had become a modern, complex, high-stress society. Big cities such as Jerusalem, Tiberius, Jericho, and Sepphoris had left behind the rustic problems of ancient Israel and entered the world of inner city slums, complex international trade, pluralistic religion (diverse Jewish groups as well as Hellenistic cults), and multicultural conflict. Contentment was no more readily available in first-century Jerusalem than in twentieth-century New York.

So Jesus was no stranger to the discontented. He lived every day among people whose lives were gnawed by sharper discontent than any we know today. If those who heard him universally lacked anything, it was contentment. What, then, does Jesus say about being content? Surprise: nothing. He never used the word. On the surface, that seems strange. Especially since virtually everyone else in the New Testament, from John the Baptist to the later Epistle writers, seems to give counsel on the subject.

John the Baptist said to the soldiers who heard his preaching of the coming kingdom of God, "Be content with your wages" (Luke 3:14). That piece of advice probably went over like management telling auto workers to quit asking for raises. The apostle Paul said to the Christians at Philippi,

> I have learned to be content with whatever I have. I know what it is to have little, and I know what it is to have plenty. In any and all

circumstances I have learned the secret of being well-fed and of going hungry, of having plenty and of being in need. (Phil 4:11-13)

The writer to the Hebrews said,

Keep your lives free from the love of money, and be content with what you have; for he has said, "I will never leave you nor forsake you." (Heb 13:5)

The author of the epistle to Timothy wrote,

Of course, there is great gain in godliness combined with contentment; for we brought nothing into the world, so that we can take nothing out of it; but if we have food and clothing, we will be content with these. (1 Tim 6:6-8)

But Jesus never used the words "content" or "contentment." Why not? Of course there is no argument from silence. But we might guess that Jesus didn't believe that telling someone to be content was the best way to bring about contentment. On the other hand, for Jesus contentment was a living concept and a daily practice. In his teachings, contentment was never a passive state, a sitting-on-the-porch-and-counting-your-money existence. To be content was to be plunged into the very midst of the activity of the reign of God. He did talk about that a lot. And it is obvious that his disciples learned contentment from him, if indirectly, when we read in the New Testament their encouragement to others to live lives of contentment. But what did Jesus understand to be contented existence?

Contentment Is Not Satisfaction with Every Condition

Jesus plainly did not understand contentment to be many of the things that religious people frequently confuse with contentment. For example, he did not think of contentment as finding satisfaction with temporal circumstances regardless of what they were. He often spoke against the widespread injustices to the poor as did the prophets before him. Contrary to custom, he included women and children in his followers. He healed the sick and handicapped. He restored lepers to society. He wept over death.

When Paul said he had learned to be content regardless of the situation (Phil 4:11), he didn't mean that every condition of life is as good as any other. He meant that he had learned to deal with the situation and not live a grumbling life during his various hardships. Paul refused to use his physical affiliations as an excuse for constantly going about in a hammered-thumb frame of mind.

When he suffered from his famous and obscure "thorn in the flesh" (2 Cor 12:7; literally, "a sharp stake"), he did not say "I have learned to enjoy life just as much with this sharp affliction, hallelujah! Thank you Jesus, for this suffering!" In fact, three times he asked God to remove the torment from his life. God's answer was no. But God did not say, "No, learn to be grateful for your misery," but rather, "No, my grace is sufficient for you, for power is made perfect in weakness" (2 Cor 12:9). Paul found meaning even in the most miserable of afflictions. But that does not mean he regarded sickness and health as equally good. Otherwise, why did he pray for his thorn in the flesh to be removed? Or, in fact, why did Jesus heal the sick?

Paul was shipwrecked three times in his life, and once "for a day and a night was adrift at sea" (2 Cor 11:25). That would be an astonishing series of adventures for anyone. In the first-century world, a ship breaking apart was probably the most terrifying situation imaginable. The sea was a negative image in the Jewish world. In the book of Revelation we are told that in the new heaven and earth "the sea was no more" (Rev 21:1). These experiences of Paul, along with the others in this litany of his hardship (1 Cor 11:23-29), certainly were regarded by him as part of his suffering. He was content to undergo it for Christ's sake and the sake of the gospel. But it was still suffering. If Paul was literally content in whatever state he was in, he never would have left the depths of the watery Mediterranean for the shore.

Contentment Is Not Passivity Toward Evil

Furthermore, contentment for Jesus did not mean passive acceptance of spiritual conditions. In fact, most of the conflict in his life came from his frequent criticism of the religious hierarchy and its practices. His "cleansing of the temple" in Jerusalem was really a dramatic and dangerous protest against the existing spiritual situation surrounding the temple. Jesus was not content with the bazaar-like atmosphere of the Temple courtyard and the accompanying problems of crooked money transactions. Foreigners, pilgrims to Jerusalem, and the poor were the victims of this injustice. As part of the peasant class in Israel,

Jesus protested against the use of the temple, a sanctuary for the oppressed, for fraud against the common people. Any religious life today that finds contentment by retreating from confrontation with ethical and moral issues is plainly not modeled after the example of Jesus.

Peter Gomes, the Plummer Professor of Christian Morals at Harvard and minister at Memorial Church, is the great-grandson of slaves. His great-grandmother triumphed over the slavery that bound her because of her inner freedom through Christ. Gomes wrote:

> When I reconsidered this, however, particularly in light of my own family's experience in this rather sordid business called slavery, I learned something. I learned it from my mother's mother's mother. . . . I learned that what made it possible for my mother's mother's mother to deal with First Timothy, [1 Tim 6:6] and the whole world in which she was brought up as a slave in Virginia, and to still embrace the Christian faith as true, authentic, authoritative, and relevant in all of its verses, not just the agreeable ones, was the notion that she already possessed in her soul that inner strength, that contentment, that freedom in Jesus Christ to which indeed the apostle here is speaking. This did not make the burdens of life any less real than they were; this did not make the pain any less disagreeable; but it certainly made it possible to retain that one thing which slavery itself could not take away: one's inner strength, one's identity, one's sense of worth and value, one's intention to survive and triumph, indeed one's contentment. . . .
>
> Contentment is not resignation. Contentment is not submission. Contentment is not simply rolling over and letting it happen. Contentment is the capacity within you not simply to survive but to prevail.[1]

The spirit of Jesus does not teach us to be content with injustices and wrongs, to simply draw our salaries and wait for our pensions. Rather, we are to prevail, to overthrow evil and replace the rule of evil with the reign of God. Gomes continued:

> Contentment, Saint Paul tells us, is to be found in the search for justice, piety, integrity, love, fortitude, gentleness. This is Paul's advice, and why? Not because these things are rewards. They are not! They are not prizes for virtuous life. They are the means to make the fundamentally unvirtuous enterprise of life manageable, bearable, and even fruitful.[2]

Contentment Is Not the Absence of Sorrow

Finally, contentment for Jesus did not mean the absence of sorrow at loss. Paul told the Corinthians not to sorrow as those who had no hope. He meant that they should not engage in wild displays of hopeless grief, not that they should not grieve at all. That unfortunate interpretation has resulted in the cruel and unnatural expectation by some pious sorts that a "real" Christian would not show sorrow at the death of someone they love. A family that remains serene, even cheerful at a funeral is frequently admired as truly Christian by the "spiritual" members of the church. On the other hand, a family in great sorrow may make these "superdisciples" uncomfortable, or even cause them to question the family's faith.

But when Lazarus, the friend of Jesus, died, Jesus was deeply affected. His earlier reaction to the death of John the Baptist also indicated that he was seriously disturbed by the event. In his struggles in the Garden of Gethsemane over his own impending death, again we are shown how seriously Jesus regarded human life and death. Life after death was a reality for Jesus and his followers, but so was death. Death, according to Revelation, is God's enemy. According to Paul, death no longer has the victory, but it still brings pain. The last enemy to be put beneath God's feet is death. If God is not content with death, regarding it as an enemy, neither should we be content. Any reaction to death that denies grief is unnatural and inconsistent with the plan of God.

A couple lost their foster son in a drowning accident at a school party. He had had a difficult life in his early years, but a new school and the love of his foster parents had transformed him. Then the tragedy occurred. The day after the accident, the mother greeted visitors to her home as if nothing had happened. She was cheerful, energetic, even buoyant. A former neighbor, a minister, had telephoned to remind her that "the Lord giveth and the Lord taketh away; blessed be the name of the Lord."

The husband sat quietly, deep in grief, as she served coffee to her guests. Finally a wild cry filled the room, shocking the visitors. The woman could restrain her emotions no longer. She stood looking toward heaven, her fists raised. "I don't care how bad you needed him, I needed him worse!" she cried. She collapsed on the sofa, and her husband tried to comfort her. Only after she had poured out her anger and grief was she able to regain her faith and her service to her church. Christian contentment plainly means something other than the denial of grief when calamities occur.

What does Jesus teach about contentment? Even though he never used the word, he dealt with the question in many ways. He showed true contentment by his simple lifestyle, his appreciation of all people regardless of their place in society, and his enjoyment of creation ("consider the flowers of the field"; "not a sparrow falls that God does not notice"). He moved easily among working people, scholars, women, outcasts, and children. He took no advantage by power or force; he envied no one and nothing. He grieved at the loss of friends, and so celebrated at joyful occasions that his enemies called him "a glutton and a drunkard." In other words, Jesus showed his contentment with being human. The primary source of evil in society, both then and now, is the attempt to deny humanity for others by making them less than human. When we do that, we also are denying humanity for ourselves by making ourselves more than human.

Jesus dealt specifically with contentment in numerous stories and sayings. For example, he told the story of the rich fool who built greater and greater barns to store his crops. He was content because his future seemed secure: "Soul, you have ample goods laid up for many years; relax, eat, drink, be merry" (Luke 12:19). But death overtook him, and all that he had stored for himself became the property of others. From this story Jesus derived one lesson: "One's life does not consist in the abundance of possessions" (v. 15). For 2,000 years this has been a difficult lesson for all of us to learn. Contentment always seems to be spelled with four letters: more. As the old farmer in Kansas once said, "I don't want all the land in the world. I just want all the land that borders mine."

Long before the Kansas farmer's day, Plutarch told of the limitless ambitions of Pyrrhus, king of Epirus (present-day Croatia and Albania). We got the term "Pyrrhic victory" from him. He was asked what he would do if his campaign to conquer Rome succeeded:

> "Why then," answers Pyrrhus, "all of Italy will fall to us." What then? inquires Cineas. "Sicily next holds out her arms to receive us," answers the enthusiastic monarch. "But will the possession of Sicily put an end to the war?" Clearly not; Libya and Carthage are the next logical victims. . . . "And when all these are in our power what shall we do then?" "We will live at our ease, my dear friend,"

responds the smiling king, "and drink all day, and divert ourselves with pleasant conversation." "And what hinders us now, sir, if we have in mind to be merry, and entertain one another, since we have at hand. . . . all those necessary things?"[3]

Contentment, for the ambitious, often is not in possessing but in dominating, conquering. That continues to be true in every century, every decade.

The 1980s became famous as a time of acquiring and exceeding. The early robber-barons of this country returned. Only this time instead of railroads and goon-squads, their implements were investment banking and leveraged buy-outs. More was never enough. Rich men went to prison for fraud, people who earned more in one year than the gross national product of most countries. But their very efforts at piling more wealth upon already enormous wealth proves the truth of Jesus' saying. If even these riches do not satisfy, then life can never be measured by wealth.

There is a life of the spirit as well as a life of the body. Wealth can make a house for the body—luxurious clothing, sumptuous banquets, magnificent mansions. But the spirit lives elsewhere. There is another world, a world of relationships with others, with creation and its creatures, with one's self.

Wealth and possessions are, in fact, more often obstacles than accesses to that life of the spirit. Only the most generous and dedicated among the rich ever succeed in the world of the spirit. Jesus warned again and again of the potential evil of material discontent. Camels go through needles' eyes easier than rich men enter the kingdom of the spirit. If one is not careful, the desire to achieve more of the abundance of things destroys more and more of the relationships of life. Relationships are rarely enhanced by wealth. People and nature must yield before the almighty bottom line.

But these greedy-to-the-last barons of business are the lucky ones. Most people who set out on that road to material riches burn out long before the end. They become exhausted climbing life's ladders, endlessly struggling upward. (Alexander the Great "wept because he had no more worlds to conquer," the legend says. Actually, there was plenty left to conquer, but in India his troops burned out.) Or to change the picture, the greedy eat so much at life's table that they lose their appetite. Hunger, as tragic and unnecessary as it is, is not the greatest disaster of life. But loss of the appetite for life is. Suicide, so prevalent in our "advanced" Western nations, is proof enough of that.

Jesus said, "Blessed (happy) are those who hunger and thirst for righteousness, for they will be filled" (Matt 5:6). Satisfaction never comes to those whose only thirst is for wealth. Wealth is like seawater. The more you drink, the thirstier you become. But it does come to those whose quest is for righteousness, life lived uprightly before God and others. A hunger for justice, equality, honest and fair dealings with others, ethical behavior on a national and even international scale, along with the acknowledgement of God as the source and substance of it all—this is a passion of the spirit that finds rich and rewarding contentment in life.

Jesus said, "Consider the lilies how they grow" (Luke 12:27). He was thinking of the brilliant, pleasant colors of the anemones that he and his disciples commonly saw blanketing the hillsides of Galilee. Even Solomon in all his finery never looked so good, Jesus said. They don't toil or spin. Yet God dresses them like that! "Consider the ravens, they neither sow nor reap," but God feeds them (v. 24).

The King James translation, "Take no thought of tomorrow" (Matt 6:34), has been misunderstood by some zealous Christians to mean that a contented Christian never plans for the future. They believe that God will make everything beautiful for us, as for the flowers, without any effort on our part. A group of solemn young Christians once were discussing a visit to one of them by an insurance salesman. "He looked like a nice guy, too, you know. But I just pointed to the Bible on my mantle and told him, 'That's my insurance!'" The others nodded sagely.

But even flowers show more adaptation to changing conditions than that. Once I tried to dig up one of those desert flowers once. Those things intend to remain in the promised land. They have developed a tap root like a live oak! That's their insurance against drought. If Jesus' analogies of toilless flowers and non-farming birds are carried too far, the flowers of the field would be rootless and the ravens would sit all day with their mouths open. Even flowers in their natural state reach with their root-fingers toward the water God provides, and birds have to use the hunt-and-peck system to eat.

Human beings have a natural life, too. As animals forage or browse for food, so human beings work. With our minds we can plan and organize so we can overcome the handicaps of seasons of cold or drought. We can also overcome the seasons of sickness, disability, old age, or infirmity with preventive medicine, exercise, and saving—with planning and providing for tomorrow.

What, then, does the Bible mean, "Take no thought"? Again, the familiar translation gives an unfortunate impression. "Do not have excessive concern" is nearer to the original meaning. In other words, "do not become preoccupied with" thoughts about tomorrow. Jesus was not teaching against planning or saving. He was urging us not to become so preoccupied with the future that we become obsessive, nervous, or distraught in our efforts at living. "Contentment," Peter Gomes says, "is that quality that puts you at ease with both what you have and what you do not have."[4] We must do what a human can do and leave the rest to God.

Jesus lived like that, and died, content in his relations with others and with God. He had only the coat on his back and the sandals on his feet. He had "nowhere to lay his head" (Matt 8:20). Only his hunger and thirst after righteousness brought him life's true contentment. We will find our contentment, if we do, only in the same way. We will never be content with the state of the world. We will likely never be content with our successes, or the lack of them. Contentment will only be ours when we seek the reign of God in our lives and our world. As Gomes said, "The essence of contentment is godliness, and the essence of godliness is inner strength because of God."[5]

Notes

[1] Peter J. Gomes, "Contentment," *Pulpit Digest* (May/June 1992): 8-9.
[2] Ibid.
[3] Eli Sagan, *The Honey and the Hemlock* (Princeton NJ: Princeton University Press, 1991) 363-64.
[4] Gomes, 5.
[5] Ibid.

Chapter 9

SYMPATHY

The Alien Becomes Family

If sympathy is a key to life, it can't be lost. Doesn't everyone have sympathy? At least for someone or something?

Certainly we don't lack sympathy for ourselves. We understand what we are trying to do and usually can find reasons to explain even the most indefensible conduct. We also understand our needs—or at least our financial obligations. As a friend once said to me, "I know everyone thinks they need to win the lottery, but I *really* need to win the lottery."

Most of us have abundant sympathy for our family members and friends. We sympathize with their aches and pains, illnesses, and misfortunes. If our little girl isn't chosen cheerleader, we suffer with her. If our son is cut from the football team, we feel his frustration and despair. Common economic interests tend to bind us together, too. Union members are sympathetic with labor and its problems; the wealthy are sympathetic to a millionaire plagued with I.R.S. audits.

Generally speaking, races also tend to sympathize with problems peculiar to themselves. An Asian businessman in California, an African-American college student in Alabama, and a Jewish doctor in Dallas all know the prejudice peculiar to their situation as minorities and sympathize with others like themselves. They may or may not, however, sympathize with one another.

The prayer of the old Scottish immigrant expressed well our limited sympathies for us and ours:

> O Lord, we come to thee today in an attitude of thanksgiving, but likewise of complaint. We came to this country expecting to find it a land flowing with milk and honey; but instead, we find it a land peopled by the ungodly Irish! O Lord, if thou hast any blessings to bestow, grant them to thine own peculiar people, the Scots. In thy infinite mercy, give them positions as policemen, magistrates, and rulers of thy people.

> But as for the ungodly Irish, O Lord, make them hewers of wood and drawers of water! Seize them by the scuff of the neck and shake them over the jaws of hell; but, O Lord, don't let them fall in, and thine shall be the honor and the glory forever. Amen.

Sympathy is a commodity in carefully regulated supply. The closer the pain to us and ours, the more likely the abundance of sympathy. But the farther the stress or suffering from our world of understanding, the shorter our supply of sympathy.

What is sympathy, anyway? Is it merely feeling sorry for someone, or vaguely wishing something bad hadn't happened to our friend or relative or fellow club member?

In some ways, sympathy is an elusive quality. In our everyday usage of the word, sympathy can refer to a variety of vague emotions. But in the life of Jesus of Nazareth, sympathy is raised to new levels of meaning. His relationships with an amazing variety of human beings put sympathy in a new light. The sympathetic life of Jesus attracted Pharisees and publicans, beggars and prostitutes, revolutionaries and children. Its powerful appeal to individuals of every race and social station has never diminished in the centuries following. Ghandi was never attracted to the Christian church, but he found the compassionate life of Jesus unique and compelling. Cheap sympathy, like cheap grace, may be common to our world. But the quality of sympathy displayed in the life of Jesus is one of the lost keys to life.

In spite of the difficulties in reconstructing the life of Jesus, the portraits of his life in the Gospels present a remarkably consistent picture of his sympathetic actions. His teachings, too, enable us to understand more fully the demands of real sympathy. In particular, he taught three parables that uniquely encompass the dimensions of sympathetic living. These are known as the parables of the wicked servant, the good Samaritan, and the prodigal son.

The Slave Who Wouldn't Forgive

The parable of the wicked servant is the story of a lucky slave who failed to learn from his own good fortune (Matt 8:23-35). He was the slave of a king and owed the king a staggering sum: 10,000 talents. Presumably these were talents of silver. We cannot accurately calculate the modern worth of 10,000 talents of silver. But according to one measure of the talent, 10,000 talents would have amounted to 959,640 pounds of silver. Therefore, the slave owed the king roughly

$65,000,000. (I wonder if they had Chapter 11 in those days?) Or put another way, a single talent was worth more than fifteen years' wages of a laborer. To repay the king, the slave would have had to work 150,000 years (and still not collect any Social Security).

The debt is obviously metaphorical. In the first place, it is unlikely that any slave, no matter how highly placed, could have gotten his hands on such a enormous sum of money or that he could have done anything to cost the king so many millions. But that is just the point. To the hearers of Jesus, themselves mostly the very poor, such a debt merely represented infinity. The slave owed infinitely.

Since the servant could not pay his debt, the king ordered him sold, along with his wife and children and what possessions he had. But the slave fell on his knees and begged the king to have patience with him—as if patience would solve his problem! The king, however, took pity on the man and forgave him the debt.

No doubt at this point the original hearers of this story were shaking their heads in amazement at such a stupendous debt, not to mention the incredible generosity of the king. Monarchs and overlords they had known would have destroyed an entire nation for that sum of money.

But the really incredible part of the story comes later. On the way out of his life-sparing audience with the king, the slave met a second slave who owed him a hundred denarii. In Jesus' day a laborer was usually paid about one Roman denarius a day. So the slave owed him 100 days' wages. That was no small sum to a slave, but even so it amounted to 500,000 times less than the debt just forgiven him by the king. Nevertheless, he grabbed his fellow slave by the throat and threatened to throttle him unless he immediately paid him what he owed him. The poor man then begged for a little time to repay his debt. But the first slave refused and had him thrown into prison "until the debt was paid." Of course, in prison he couldn't repay the debt. His fate was sealed.

His fellow servants then entered the story. They knew of the king's amazing generosity to the first slave and were outraged at his unsympathetic treatment of the man who owed him a comparably small sum. So they told the king of this injustice, and the king reacted predictably. He summoned the man whom he had forgiven and called him wicked and hardhearted. The king asked if he, the servant, should not have forgiven his fellow slave in light of the forgiveness of his own huge debt. He then ordered the man delivered to the torturers until he paid his entire debt. (Unless sweat-equity counts, he's going to be there awhile.) Not a pretty outcome, but kings in that time were not pretty people.

The point of the story does not need amplification. The picture is plain enough. The king generously turned an unpayable debt into a payable one. The slave wickedly turned a payable debt into an unpayable one. Such lack of sympathy is inhuman and results in dire consequences for the inhuman person, or nation, that practices it. The generosity of God, even to the infinite debtor, is the good news of this parable of Jesus. But our unsympathetic treatment of one another receives a stern warning.

The Sympathetic Samaritan

The second story about sympathetic living, known as the parable of the good Samaritan (Luke 10:25-37), is more familiar. The Samaritans and Jews of Jesus' day had become bitter enemies over several centuries. After Alexander the Great conquered Israel (332 B.C.), the residents of the city of Samaria rebelled. One of Alexander's generals put down the rebellion and expelled the citizens of Samaria, subsequently building a Hellenistic city on the site. The Samaritans fled to the ruins of the ancient city of Shechem, which they rebuilt.

Later they built a temple on nearby Mount Gerazim and established their own worship. The Samaritans followed the teaching of the Torah alone, the first five books of the Bible. They had their own priesthood and believed that the worship at the temple in Jerusalem was corrupt. In turn, the Samaritans were forbidden by the Jews from worshiping in the temple. Both Jews and Samaritans avoided contact with one another, and each regarded the other as heretics.

The parable was prompted by a lawyer who asked Jesus to give the requirements for eternal life. Jesus then asked him what the Law said. When the lawyer replied that the law required wholehearted love of God and neighbor (Lev 19:18), Jesus agreed. Do those things, he said, and you shall live. But then the lawyer asked specifically who constituted his neighbor.

Leviticus 19:18 presupposes fellow Israelites alone as neighbors. Verses 33-34, however, include resident aliens also: "You shall love the alien as yourself, for you were aliens in the land of Egypt." Debates over such scriptures were common in Israel in the first century, and the lawyer likely was asking Jesus' opinion of the extent of the laws regulating conduct toward a neighbor. If eternal life was dependent upon not cheating, despising, or slandering a neighbor; not coveting a neighbor's wife or possessions; or not charging interest or withholding loans from a neighbor, then just who was a neighbor?

Jesus' answer had to have been astonishing to the lawyer. He told a parable about a man traveling the most notoriously bad stretch of road in the region, the road from Jerusalem to Jericho. That precipitous, downhill highway harbored thieves and murderers along its rocky flanks. When Jesus began his story by saying, "A man was going from Jerusalem to Jericho," the story struck a minor chord, and cold chills likely went down more than one spine. When he further said, "and [he] fell into the hands of robbers," heads everywhere probably nodded and one person nudged another. Of course. What else could a traveler expect on that road?

Then a priest and a Levite (the lesser order of priests in the temple) passed by without aiding the stripped and battered victim at the side of the road. They were merely exercising prudent conduct. After all, thieves were known to fake such injuries to lure people close enough for assault. (They still do. A prostrate man in the access lane of Interstate-4 in Florida was arrested for attempting to lure motorists to stop and render aid. He was found with a pistol in his possession.) These two religious persons passed by, cautiously, "on the other side." Wry smiles and nods came again from the audience. No help from the temple crowd; they were looking out for themselves.

Then came the real shock. A Samaritan passed by, and seeing the wounded man he was moved with sympathy. He poured soothing oil and anaseptic wine on the victim's wounds and bandaged them. Then he placed the man on his own animal and brought him to an inn, where he watched beside him overnight. The next day the Samaritan paid the innkeeper to take care of the injured man until he returned, and he promised to repay whatever other expenses he had incurred.

"Which of these was a neighbor?" Jesus asked. "The Samaritan," said the lawyer. No, he didn't say that—not exactly. The lawyer could not bring himself even to say the word Samaritan. "The one who showed him mercy," the lawyer said. "Right," Jesus said. "Now go and do the same."

Likely many former camp followers went home after that, ruefully shaking their heads: "That Jesus! He's just too liberal for me. Of all the ways he could have said it, why did he have to use the word Samaritan! I mean, the point could have been made without whitewashing those no-good, God-dishonoring heretics!"

But Jesus had made exactly the point he intended. The neighbor was not the expected Israelite, but the despised Samaritan. Yet neighbor is a reciprocal term; it takes two for the neighbor concept to function. The unknown, unnamed, race-undesignated, religion-unspecific, faceless stranger by the roadside became the neighbor of the Samaritan. The lawyer wanted to know the limits of his responsibility. As far as he was concerned, the circle of neighbors, with its obligations, couldn't get too small for him. Jesus refused to define neighbor, that is, those we are obligated to help. Rather, he defined the neighbor-relationship: anyone, anywhere, in need, faceless, raceless, religionless—whatever—and anyone who cares to help become neighbors.

"Who proved to be a neighbor?" Jesus asked. The stranger who cared, and whose caring took on hands and feet and money and follow-up, that one proved to be neighbor. In other words, our neighborhood has no limits. No streets mark its boundaries; no covenants define its inhabitants. The duties of neighbor transcend legal obligations, civil or religious. The priest and Levite were both scrupulous observers of the codes of propriety of that time. Yet they had no sympathy for the battered man beside the road. Their concern for themselves and their limited definition of neighbor exempted them from their obvious obligations as fellow members of the human race. Sympathy, then, in this second parable of Jesus is never restricted to any one neighborhood. It is a citizen of the world.

The Father Who Understood Two Sons

The final story is perhaps the best-known parable ever told. It is the story of the prodigal son (Luke 15:20). A boy demanded his inheritance from his well-to-do father. He wished to go out and see the world on his own. According to the Law, the father wasn't obligated to give his wealth away before his death. Nevertheless, this man was an understanding father, and he did so. The boy then promptly ran away to a far city and wasted his inheritance on wine, women, and song.

At this point in the story, the listeners—undoubtedly overwhelmingly if not exclusively male—would have been shaking their heads in disgust. Of course! What else could the father expect? Anyone so foolish as to give this selfish boy whatever he wished deserved what he got! No wonder the boy turned out the way he did! Such an indulgent father would spoil any child.

Having spent his last nickel, the boy lost his last friend. When he had bought the final round of drinks, he had bought his last companion. Destitute, the boy was reduced to tending pigs. Nothing could be more unimaginably loathsome to a Jew. (Obviously, this nasty job was in pagan territory, since Jews didn't raise pigs.) Finally, the boy was starving. His master would give him nothing. He ate the rough carob-pods that were the pigs' fodder.

Then, crawling in the mire, fighting with the pigs over their food, the boy suddenly saw himself. In a rare moment of self-understanding, he stood on his two feet and knew who he was. Even the servants of his father had plenty to eat, and he was starving. He left the pigs and their heartless owner behind. But knowing that he had wronged his father and disgraced himself, he practiced his homecoming speech. He would confess that he had "sinned against heaven and before you" and was no more worthy to be called his father's son. He only wished to be a hired servant.

But this father, again, was not predictable. He should have allowed the village elders to put the boy to death for taking his wealth prematurely. Instead, he ran to greet the boy, an unseemly act for a dignified Jewish elder. Perhaps he wanted to avoid the possibility that the men of the village might seize the boy first. When his son began his speech of contrition, the father did a series of astonishing things.

He ordered his servants to fetch the best robe, a festal garment, and a ring—signifying authority—for the boy's hand. But the most telling gesture may have been his final command. He ordered sandals brought for his son's feet. Slaves didn't wear sandals. Finally, he ordered a fatted calf to be killed for a celebration. The father then declared the boy to be his son, not his hired hand. The one who "was dead has come to life," he proclaimed; "he was lost and has been found!"

In this great story the father's sympathy stands at its center. Clearly, the parable does not focus on the boy, the "prodigal son," whose conduct was typical and predictable. Its focus is on the father, whose reactions were anything but typical. (Helmut Thielicke calls this story, "the parable of the Waiting Father.") He understood that to live by law was to lose the boy. He knew the boy's restlessness and his desire for autonomy. His intuitive understanding led him to the right decision, as painful as it proved for both of them. Then when the boy returned, all legalism was laid aside in the pure joy of reunion. The father felt the boy's anguish and humiliation; he knew that no further indignities were necessary.

But this is really not the end of the story, though the prodigal's adventures and return are its most familiar parts. An elder brother was also at home, and he became indignant when he heard of the celebration for the prodigal. His actions, too, were typical. He began to sulk and refused to go into the house. Finally the father came out to him, as he did for his brother, and pled for the elder son to join the celebration. But the older son angrily refused. For years he had worked like a slave for the father, he said, and yet he never was given so much as a goat for a barbecue. He never disobeyed one order, but when the son who "devoured your property with prostitutes" returned, a fatted calf was killed! The father insisted that all he had belonged to the elder brother and that they had always been together. "But we had to celebrate and rejoice, because this brother of yours was dead and has come to life; he was lost and has been found."

The elder brother revealed the kind of self-centered life that cannot love, and cannot understand love when it sees it. He called his brother "this son of yours"; the father reminded him that the prodigal was also "this brother of yours." Jesus was showing that the father was not the only one who had the responsibility of sympathetic conduct. The outraged man who paced back and forth outside the house ablaze with light was also the brother of the humiliated son who had returned. The father's sympathy for the elder brother caused him to go out into the night in an effort to reconcile that son, too, to the family. Even the "righteous," Jesus was saying, have a responsibility to sympathize and celebrate with the return of prodigals.

Donald Juel reminds us, as Christian brothers and sisters, that this parable is part of the context of the Lord's Prayer:

> The Lord's Prayer should be heard in the context of a story that is about conflict, alienation, and reconciliation. . . . Such a prayer is

unthinkable as long as bitterness and smoldering resentment can be rekindled by the very graciousness that allows a place for prodigals. Such a prayer is possible only if liberation of another sort can be experienced—only if bondage to resentment can be broken, a bondage that masks itself as virtue and concern for justice. The elder children will be able to ask for forgiveness and extend it to others only if God's forgiveness extends to them, the pious and the pious and responsible, . . . whose sin is the inability to forgive God for being gracious to the ungodly.[1]

In each of these three parables, human sympathy is tried by an adversary and a conflict situation. We wouldn't expect sympathy to be shown in any of them. The wicked servant, perhaps through fraud, owed a gigantic, unpayable sum. Who would forgive that? The good Samaritan was in Jewish territory when he saw an assault victim who had already been bypassed by two officials of the temple. Who would expect him to become "the stupid Samaritan" and risk caring for a Jew? The prodigal son had taken advantage of a loving father and wasted his money "stupidly." Should the father forgive this no-good?

The point is, the kind of sympathy Jesus taught is anything but casual, cheap, or shallow. It cannot be achieved by mere sentimentalism or occasional coins of charity. "Tea and sympathy" may be expected among polite society, but the sympathy shown in these parables is scarcely the idle sort murmured over a saucer at four o'clock tea. This kind of sympathy calls for the deepest and strongest impulses of the human spirit.

An ancient king could do as he pleased with someone who owed such a debt as the wicked servant. But the king in the parable had mercy on him and forgave a debt he knew could never be repaid. A Samaritan had no reason to risk his own neck to rescue and care for a wounded traveler on a road in Judea, but he bound his wounds and paid for his care. A Jewish father of the first century had no obligation to readmit such a failed, ruined child as this prodigal son into his house. But this good father understood the boy's remorse and lavishly celebrated his return.

These individuals in Jesus' parables followed a higher law than any set down in the rules of society. At the same time, we are shown the opposite conduct from others. The wicked servant turned on a debtor for a pittance and showed him no mercy at all. A priest and a Levite forgot their obligations to a stranger and went about their own business, leaving the victim on the road to die. The elder brother pouted and fussed over his wounded ego and could not understand his father's love for a ruined brother. Is it not unfortunately true that such attitudes are more to be expected in our world than their opposite?

What Does It Mean To Be Sympathetic?
To be sympathetic not only means to "feel together with" someone or something. More specifically, it means "to be partisan to" the interests or needs of someone.

An Indianapolis judge recently wept openly at the testimony of a woman who was raped, shot at, and beaten with a revolver. Carol Kleiman of the *Chicago Tribune* called it "a watershed event" for the U.S. judicial system. When the judge sentenced the rapist to eighty years in prison, defense attorneys appealed and asked for the judge's removal, claiming that the judge showed bias toward the victim. The judge was a woman, Paula Lapossa. Her "reprehensible behavior" was described as "conspicuous compassion." The *New York Times* said the judge did not weep at the testimony of the rape assault, but at "the victim's forgiving nature." The Indiana Court of appeals ultimately denied the appeal, saying tears did not necessarily indicate bias.

If sympathy is removed summarily from life's courtroom—ours included—who won't be a victim? "Conspicuous compassion" is a great term for a Christian attribute we all should extend to the worlds we live in. "To be partisan to" those who suffer is the very definition of sympathy.

Like the old Scottish immigrant, we don't have a problem being partisan to our own causes. Nor did the wicked servant, the priest or Levite, or the elder brother. But have we not seen ourselves in them and their self-centeredness? The point of these parables is the need for us all to be partisan to one another regardless of party, race, or business interests, simply as fellow human beings, members of the same human community. These stories say, God is like that. These stories say, we can be like that, too.

We are given a few clues to gaining this sort of understanding, God's sort of sympathy. In the first of these parables, the story of the wicked servant, we are shown that the mercy of the great king should have prompted the servant to do likewise. But he learned nothing from the king's example. His killer instinct soon emerged, and his remorseless treatment of his fellow slave led to his own destruction. For those of us who believe God is active in this world, the story is a reminder of God's repeated forgiveness for all of humankind's debts and our need to forgive others likewise. Whether someone believes in God or not, can anyone doubt that without this kind of sympathetic hearing of one another, without giving one another a second chance, our world hasn't got a chance? Can we doubt that we all eventually will be delivered to the tormentors? And that those tormentors are in fact ourselves, even those of our own house? Seen in that light, sympathy is clearly not just a pastel virtue for afternoon tea. It is an essential ingredient to future life on this planet.

In the story of the good Samaritan, we are shown that sympathy means belief in mutual human need rather than in human superiority. The Samaritan did not allow questions of race, religion, or social class to decide his merciful action. He remembered the times when he was needy, often wounded by others, and he went to the side of someone else who was suffering.

In the 1950s, a reporter from a Shreveport, Louisiana, newspaper went across the state line to Marshall, Texas, to conduct an experiment. He posed as a severely handicapped person and sat begging on the sidewalk at the courthouse square. At the end of the day, he had come to one conclusion. Though he was white, white people almost without exception passed him by without giving him anything. Black people almost without exception put a few coins in his cup. The reporter concluded that those who gave to him could identify with his need. They were partisan to his problems.

Superiority is a disastrous attitude. Wherever human beings feel themselves superior, sympathy is impossible. At best, pity, a second-hand emotion, takes over; at worst, disgust is the result. But superiority forgets its own dependence on others. Superiority forgets the helping hands of the past and its many birthrights and inheritances, social as well as physical, that allowed for superior feelings in the first place. When one element of society looks down on another, suffering for both groups eventually will only be magnified.

The great parable of the prodigal son, the third of Jesus' lessons on sympathy, suggests something about understanding and sympathy. The father showed a belief in a dynamic rather than a static view of life. He understood his son's struggle toward autonomy in a home with a successful father and a dominant, demanding elder brother. He also believed that his son would overcome his immaturity and grow into a wiser man. There was tremendous risk in his gamble. But he stood ready to accept the son back into his world when and if the son "came to himself."

Much of our lack of sympathy is really due to a short memory. Were not most over-demanding mothers and fathers once headstrong children themselves? And have we not all made colossal mistakes in judgment, mistakes that well could have ruined us permanently if it had not been for someone who believed we could change? Without such a sympathetic understanding of life by someone in our past, the majority of us would be derelict in this world.

A young man once was brought before the discipline committee of a seminary. The decision of the committee could mean his expulsion from the school, and likely the end of his efforts toward ministry. In rebellion against certain decisions of the school, he had written anonymous letters that were severely critical of its policies to the trustees. These actions had landed him before the committee.

After the hearing, the vote seemed certain. The student admitted his actions, and though contrite about his methods, he held firmly to his opinions. Just before the vote was taken, one professor spoke. He was regarded as a stern, strict man, though a man of great principle. In a soft voice, he told of an experience as a freshman in college.

He had a part-time job as a sexton in a church not of his own denomination. The job was essential to his staying in school. He heard of a conference to be held in the church on a theme with which his denomination strongly disagreed. The night before the conference he placed on every pew handbills that attacked the views of the speaker. The college was sponsored by the denomination of that church, and he was quickly brought before its discipline committee. One professor on the committee recognized his actions as those of an overzealous, immature young man. He insisted that such a beginning was not altogether bad, and that his zeal could lead eventually to forthright and courageous ministry. The student was allowed to stay in school.

When the vote at the seminary was taken, the committee decided unanimously that the student should be given another chance. The sympathy shown years before for the professor became the key to his life of service. Through his understanding, it also became the key to a second chance for another struggling student.

Sympathy

The sympathy taught in these three parables can lead each of us to the kind of compassionate action that inevitably transforms human life. When we come to recognize all human faces as family members, we become partisan to their experience. Henri Nouwen wrote:

> Through compassion it is possible to recognize man's craving for love in our own heart and his cruelty in our own impulses; to see our hope for forgiveness in our friend's eyes and our refusal in their bitter mouths. When they kill, we know that we could have done it; when they give life, we know that we can do the same.[2]

This kind of understanding would cause us to tear down every wall and abandon every clique that separates us from one another. There could be no more barriers, in fact as well as theory, between rich and poor, educated and uneducated, nation and nation, class and class. As a family, humankind would move toward that ideal society in which, as Isaiah put it,

> The wolf shall lie with the lamb, the leopard shall lie down with the kid, the calf and the lion and the fatling together, and a little child shall lead them. The cow and the bear shall graze, their young shall lie down together; and the lion shall eat straw like the ox. The nursing child shall play over the hole of the asp, and the weaned child shall put its hand on the adder's den. They will not hurt or destroy on all my holy mountain; for the earth will be full of the knowledge of the LORD as the waters cover the sea. (11:6-9)

A fantasy? Not really. We have all seen pictures of mother cats that have adopted baby ducks, or gorillas that have adopted kittens. But that only happens when the alien outsider becomes family. When such an adoption occurs, the biblical ideal for creation is realized. Humans, though not always the brightest of God's creatures, can do it, too.

Nouwen sees our generation as hostile to authority and particularly resentful of all "father figures," including the church. Nevertheless, we continue to look for the assurance, security, and absolution that was once provided by such authoritarian structures. According to Nouwen, we need brothers and sisters who can stand beside us, rather than authority figures that tower over us, to lead us toward forgiveness and understanding.

A fatherless generation looks for brothers who are able to take away their fear and anxiety, who can open the doors of their narrow-mindedness and show them that forgiveness is a possibility which dawns on the horizon of humanity.[3]

You Shall Love the Alien as Yourself

Both Christians and Jews hold this commandment as the highest measure of sympathy: "You shall love your neighbor as yourself" (Lev 19:18; Mark 12:31). Unfortunately, history has shown that neither faith has been as attentive to the other words in the Bible that initially accompanied this injunction.

> When an alien resides with you in your land, you shall not oppress the alien. The alien who resides with you shall be to you as the citizen among you; *you shall love the alien as yourself,* for you were aliens in the land of Egypt: I am the LORD your God. (Lev 19:33-34)

Because the Israelites had been aliens in Egypt, they were expected to empathize with others in the same situation. Paul likewise reminded Christians that as Gentiles they were once aliens and strangers, outsiders to the kingdom of God (Eph 2:12).

How different Western history would have been if this principle had been consistently practiced! Most of our wars have been fought by insiders against outsiders. The Jews in Europe and America were persecuted as undesirable aliens. African-Americans, Asians, Hispanics, and even Native Americans continue to suffer discrimination because they are regarded as "alien" to the white majority. And in modern Israel the "resident aliens," the Palestinians, are regarded as unwanted aliens in their own homeland. Yet, as Nouwen wrote, "For a compassionate man nothing human is alien: no joy and no sorrow, no way of living and no way of dying."[4]

To identify in active sympathy with outsiders, to be partisan to their needs, is costly. The church hesitated to do it with Jews in Germany, to its shame. Again in the South, in South Africa, and in Latin America, the church's sympathies were with the powerful and well-to-do majorities. The minorities were put under scriptures such as the "curse of Ham" or the biblical household code for slaves.

A president of the Southern Baptist Convention once said that God does not hear the prayer of Jews. At the beginning of the civil rights era, the same person addressed the South Carolina legislature to affirm the godliness of its segregation. Later he repented of these and similar remarks—just as soon as popular opinion had swung in the opposite direction. In June of 1995, the Southern Baptist Convention officially "repented" of its Civil War attitudes, keeping intact its record of remaining at least two generations safely behind the moral opinion of secular society.

Until the church begins to lead culture toward godly sympathies rather than waiting until it is safe to do so, it will never be regarded as more than the lap-dog of the bosses of culture. Allen Boesak, who witnessed the wrong sympathies of the dominant South African church, wrote of the same situation in South America:

> In Colombia the son of a farm laborer—a squatter on a rich man's estate, where people work and live like slaves, and eat mud in winter to survive, and die of it—this youth said in answer to a question: "God is the friend of generals and bishops, and he dines with the landowner." In his experience God belonged with the rich, with violence, with the "church." In his experience, they were all the same.
>
> It is not a new problem: it seems to many that throughout history God has all too often appeared in the garb of the rich and the privileged, standing on the side of the authorities and without protest abiding by all the untruths, the half-truths, and the equivocating myths. In South Africa, God is white and he votes for the Nationalist Party. Just as he blessed the weapons of the Boer commandos a century-and-a-half ago, so today he blesses the weapons of the riot police. And a clergyman who became a cabinet minister can say without blushing: "To be an Afrikaner is to be white and Afrikaans-speaking. . . . on the side of right and just, and on the side of God."[5]

Christians have feared such people, and with good reason. Churches have been bombed; children killed; synagogues torched; and godly leaders arrested, jailed, and executed for having the wrong sympathies. Jesus was killed for the same reason. His sympathies lay in the wrong direction.

Even a close brush with that kind of hatred can be terrifying. I sat up all one Saturday night in the 1960s with my neighbor in his front yard because a cross had just been burned in front of his house. I had awakened to the flames of the cross and the sight of this little shoe salesman sitting under a mimosa tree with a rifle across his lap. Three times I left him to call the police as again and again a white automobile circled ominously through our quiet neighborhood. No one came to help.

That morning as the salesman had gone into the shop where he worked, he saw a Klan poster calling for a rally. He tore the sign from the telephone pole and threw it into a trash can on the street. One man saw him do it. Within an hour he was receiving threatening, anonymous calls: "You nigger lover! If you don't put that sign back up, we're going to burn your house down." I didn't know what to do as I sat beside him. Over and over he said nervously to me, "I don't think I could shoot anybody. But I can't let them burn my house and kill my family."

Finally, frightened and enraged, I went back to the parsonage and called the city mayor, who was a member of our church. I told him no one had come from the police station, and that if no one came soon, the next morning I would walk out of the pulpit and across the street to the steps of the courthouse where I would preach the damndest sermon ever heard in that town. Within ten minutes, a patrol car arrived. There was no further trouble.

We are afraid with good reason. But it is easier to act in these dramatic situations than in the everyday intimidations to our Christian sympathies. I also stood in a men's store in the same town and said nothing one day when I heard a salesman tell a black man that a pair of socks cost ten dollars. They really cost two dollars. He was surprised, but he left quietly. No black had ever bought anything there. As I left (never to return), I heard the salesman say, "They'll always cost $10.00 to those black S.O.B.s."

To contradict the partisanships in our churches that really matter to people—blood issues, money and place issues—is to risk our friendships, our livelihood, our future. We say we would risk our lives for the faith. But could that be true, when we will not risk the loss of a pulpit, a friend, or even an unpleasant response?

Dietrich Bonhoeffer, who paid the ultimate price for his sympathies, wrote:

> We are not Christ, but if we want to be Christians, we must have some share in Christ's large-heartedness by acting with responsibility and in freedom when the hour of danger comes, and by showing

ns, but by the sufferings of his brethren, for whose sake Christ suffered.[6]

a real sympathy that springs, not from fear, but from the liberating and redeeming love of Christ for all who suffer. Mere waiting and looking on is not Christian behavior. The Christian is called to sympathy and action, not in the first place by his own sufferings, but by the sufferings of his brethren, for whose sake Christ suffered.[6]

Sympathy, as the Jewish and Christian Scriptures teach it, and as Bonhoeffer lived it, is no irrelevant emotion. It is a way of life. It forms the foundation of the kingdom of God on earth.

Notes

[1] Donald Juel, *The Lord's Prayer in the Gospels of Matthew and Luke*, ed. Daniel L. Migliore (Grand Rapids MI: Eerdmans, 1993) 64, 69.

[2] Henri Nouwen, "Generation without Fathers," *Search for Silence*, ed. Elizabeth O'Connor (Waco TX: Word, 1972) 62.

[3] Ibid.

[4] Ibid.

[5] Allen Boesak, "Presence of the Hidden God," *The Finger of God* (Maryknoll NY: Orbis Books, 1982) 33.

[6] Dietrich Bonhoeffer, *Letters and Papers from Prison*, ed. Eberhard Bethge, trans. Reginald Fuller (New York: Macmillan, 1971) 13-14.

Chapter 10

TOUCH

The Hands of Jesus

Quiet horror stories are always the worst. The loud, brutal stories of aggression get the headlines, but the quiet, gray ones of neglect are the most chilling.

A poor woman in Southern California who lived alone wrote to a newspaper columnist to ask how she could get some of that junk mail everyone complained about. She never got any mail at all, she said, and it would be nice to have something in her mail box each day to look forward to.

In the Stockholm suburb of Traneberg, an eighty-four-year-old woman was found dead on the balcony of her apartment two months after she had frozen to death, apparently while watching New Year's fireworks. She was still sitting in her chair, dressed in a coat and hat, her head down against the balcony railing. A neighbor called police after watching her for several days and noticing she never moved.

In Deltona, Florida, a seventy-six-year-old man was taken to a hospital for mental observation after neighbors complained of the odor from his house. He was found living alone with his dog and upwards of 400 rats. According to the man who cut his grass, he seemed lonely: "He'd talk your arm off if you said something to him." Police said the dog and rats were in good shape. The man fed them both dog food. Apparently nobody bothered anybody. The rats seemed tame, the police said; "They were real fat and healthy. They had thick fur and just sat and looked at us when we went in." The man said they were his friends.

Why doesn't somebody write to the poor woman who is hungry for mail, even junk mail? Why does it take two months for somebody to notice a dead woman who sits around the clock on an apartment balcony in freezing weather? Why did she have to watch the New Year begin, and her old life end, by herself, without a human touch? And why does an old man take better care of his rats than the neighbors take of him?

Touch

A touch is usually regarded as insignificant, the least of all human encounters. That's especially so in our crowded world. Shopping malls, schools, stadiums, and state fairs are all crowded. Who doesn't hate crowds? We are bumped, jostled, and shoved from sunup to sundown.

If we think about being touched at all, it's usually to avoid it. In New York, and in many other big American cities, even eye contact is dangerous. Strangers resent being touched by other strangers, and sometimes eye contact on a crowded sidewalk or subway can be a fatal mistake. So who wants to be touched anymore? All of us.

The fearful, crowded world in which we live only increases our loneliness and isolation. Our fear of the masses makes us more solitary. The meaningless daily jostling makes us more needy of a meaningful touch. Men and women get into empty liaisons and affairs, or drug themselves, or throw themselves into any other of a thousand useless hopes because they need some meaningful human touch and don't know where to find it, or even if such a thing exists anymore, God help them.

If you read the Bible cover to cover, you'll wonder at first if even God is interested in helping the lonely. God is the Almighty in the Old Testament all right, but back then God didn't seem to be very much into touching. I could find less than a half-dozen references to God touching anyone in the Old Testament. Now "smite," that's a big word in the Old Testament. Over 300 times we are told that God smote something or someone. "The fear of the Lord is the beginning of knowledge" (Prov 1:7). True enough, but in Old Testament times it must have been the beginning of running for cover, too.

In the New Testament, the word "touch" suddenly blossoms. Jesus' primary contact with others was through touch. He touched children, widows, beggars, the blind, the sick of every description, even lepers. Jesus went out of his way to touch the untouchables of society. Most often they were strangers. He rarely saw any of them again, which means he knew they couldn't do anything for him.

Sometimes accidentally, more often deliberately, Jesus touched all people who weren't important enough even to get junk mail: such as women, who couldn't testify in court, much less vote, or be educated, or follow rabbis around; children, who had no power anyway; the poor, who could only beg, and who had all of life stacked against them; and of course, the unclean, such as lepers, who lived outside of every warm circle of human society and whose pollution meant they couldn't attend worship. Jesus touched even prostitutes, whose moral uncleanness meant that none of the "morally superior" ever touched them—except, of course, to buy them with money.

These were the people Jesus touched. Perhaps more than anything else—his teaching, his preaching, even his miracles—this all-inclusive touch accounts for the overwhelming response of ordinary people to Jesus, both in his lifetime and in all of the centuries following.

Reach Out? Me?

The Christlike touch is often missing in our society today. Many of us have complained about the lack of a personal touch in medicine. House calls and the kindly old country doctor have been replaced by waiting rooms where you take a number and wait your turn for a three-minute quickie with a doctor who looks like he just ran in with a Doberman behind him (intermediate visit: $45). HMOs are sworn to getting you in and out of the hospital with as little contact as possible with anybody except practical nurses, low-tech equipment (such as bed pans), and basic medicine (two aspirin: $4.00).

Some doctors and medical schools are well aware of these complaints. They realize that the personal touch is essential to the healing process. Dr. David Eisenberg of Harvard Medical School, who was featured on Bill Moyers' television documentary, "Healing and the Mind," said: "I take joy in medicine, and try to know people as fully as I can, as persons, apart from their diseases." He tries to convey this to patients and teach it to medical students. He believes that if students don't learn this, "they'll be unfulfilled and won't be as good providers as they could be."[1]

Touch is not only missing in those dramatic newspaper stories of neglect or abuse, or in cold public hospitals. Our lack of touch is also evident in the countless, thoughtless ways we live our crazy lives.

I sat in the coffee shop of a large seminary one winter afternoon and watched the young apprentice preachers as they came and went. All of the booths were filled with energetic ministers-to-be; optimism and idealism had virtually displaced all the oxygen from the room.

From time to time during the hour, I watched a slight woman of more than retirement age who quietly served the tables. Her face was soft and white and powdery, and her mouth never lost its gentle smile.

Touch

No one noticed her. No one spoke to her, not once in the hour; no one said "Thanks" or "How are you?" or "It's a nice day, isn't it?"

She didn't seem to mind. She enjoyed the young preachers-in-waiting, their young lives full of promise, hope, spirituality, and utter blindness. She was from Lithuania, and her life story at least would have made a useful sermon illustration for them, someday, if they had learned it. When I said hello to her, her wonderful, surprised smile made me feel ashamed and hypocritical as I thought of the days I had come there before I noticed her.

All of us fail to give the personal touch. Robert Coles, a Harvard professor, psychiatrist, and sociologist, had the same sort of experience at Harvard:

> I knew [a woman once] who worked as a food server in a Harvard dormitory, and later, as a waitress in the august Harvard Faculty Club.... Once, when talking about Harvard, she mentioned all the teaching and learning that take place there, and took pains to emphasize the importance and value of such achievements. But she saw a darker side to life around her at work, which she once described to me this way: "I see lots of good folks here, kids trying to learn all they can, and teachers trying to teach the best they can; but there's lots of big-shots, stuffed shirt folks here, and boy, do they sell themselves hard, and boy, do they do lots of strutting and conniving, and boy, are they the worst to go near and try to serve."
>
> She'll never write an article or a book or a monthly column for a magazine, but all of us in Cambridge and other such high and mighty places the world over might try remembering the lesson she has learned about us as we contemplate the place where we are, the life that we are living, the destination we hope someday to achieve.[2]

If we do contemplate our lives, what do we find? Sometimes, I guess, we are just careless. My young seminarians who had eyes to see, but saw not, were not malicious in their oversight. They were simply so full of themselves and their own stories, like most of us most of the time, they could not focus on anyone else.

On the other hand, sometimes such blindness, such absence of the human touch, indicates a deep character flaw, an intentional looking away from anyone "inferior" to ourselves. More often, I think, it indicates a conscious effort to ignore anyone whose needs might claim our valuable time or money. These days, the poor aren't the only ones who fall into the latter category. The elderly in our world increasingly are forced to live without a loving touch.

Reuters News Service recently reported a new business that has sprung up in Japan to compensate for the neglect of the elderly by their children and relatives. Satsuki Oiwa began a rent-a-family service in Tokyo, called Japan Efficiency Corporation, which can provide a "family" for lunch and a few hours of conversation for the parents of busy business people. All a lonely old person has to do is dial the company and ask for the person he or she is missing: a son or a daughter, perhaps, or both of them, or their grandchildren. The stand-ins, who are all part-time actors, "will show up at your door and greet you emotionally as if they hadn't seen you for years." The cost for three hours with your temporary family: $1130, plus transportation costs. It would be cheaper to get the real family. But of course, that's the point, isn't it? They won't come. Satsuki Oiwa says, "What is common about our clients is that they are thirsty for human love."

So is the whole world. At least these old people have the money to hire pretended love, and somewhere they have miserable relatives to feel guilty about their neglect. Society at least still feels sorry for them and writes news articles about them half a world away. What about the others? Who cares about them? The ones nobody feels sorry for, the ones that "fall through the cracks"? And the cracks in our society seem to grow wider election by election.

The Untouchables

One of Jesus' best known parables describes a "forgotten" person. A beggar named Lazarus once was laid by his friends at a rich man's gate, Jesus said, describing a familiar scene. Where else could they put him, anyhow? There were no relief societies, no social agencies to help. The beggar was just hoping to get the table scraps the rich man threw out, and maybe a coin or two on holidays.

The rich man had a problem. If the beggar was crippled, the rich man was blind—willfully, intentionally blind. Each day he tried not to see the heap of human rags who sat at his door, and one day he didn't have to try anymore. The rich man finally noticed Lazarus no more than he noticed the mezuza on his doorpost. He never put anything into Lazarus's tin cup, except once. One morning when he was exceptionally hung over and in a foul mood, he flipped the butt of his breakfast cigarette into the cup and told the beggar to get the hell away from his gate. Who could blame him? The beggar wasn't his personal welfare project. Why should he put up with him, much less give him money?

Jesus said the dogs came and licked his ulcerated sores, this beggar named Lazarus. He had no strength to fend them off. That was the only touch he received at Mr. Big's gate.

But the rich man knew the Scripture—at least the part of it he believed. Didn't Deuteronomy 28 say plainly that those who obeyed God would be blessed materially while the disobedient would go without? Well, who was obviously the Lord's favorite here? And who was enduring whatever punishment he deserved in life? Those stern words from the prophets that said the rich were obligated to share with the poor—Isaiah called them "your own kin"—of course, the rich man ignored (Isa 58:6-7).

Like it or not, these "insignificant" people, the poor Lazarus's of the world, define us. As this story makes abundantly clear, our destinies are forever bound to theirs; we cannot achieve true paradise while they are in torment. Those who are laid at our gates today—whatever their degree of poverty, handicap, suffering, need, or powerlessness—also are our responsibility, we who have been blessed in life. As the rich like us have learned over the centuries in many bitter lessons, neglecting those at our gates eventually leads to hell, later if not sooner.

The greatest preacher to the court of the golden monarch of France, Louis XIV, "the Sun King," was none of the famous orators of France. Neither the eloquent Bossuet or Bourdaloue nor the saintly Fenelon held that distinction. The most prophetic voice ever to challenge any court was a plain priest, Father Jean Baptiste Massillon. For his first sermon before the king and his giddy, indulgent court he chose the text, "Blessed are those who mourn" (Matt 5:4). That was only a warm-up. After that, he preached repeatedly to that aristocratic court against the corruption of the French nobility and their neglect of the poor.

Massillon preached his most prophetic sermon, "On Charity," only eighty years before the storming of the Bastille by the French peasants. In it he warned the rich of the impending disaster that would fall on them and all of France if they did not heed the cries of the poor:

> Could we investigate the source of their [the French nobility's] misfortunes; if their ashes . . . could speak, what would they say to us, these sad marks of our grandeur? "It is the tears of the poor, whom we neglected, whom we oppressed, which have gradually sapped, and at last have totally overthrown them: their cries have drawn down the thunder of Heaven upon our palaces. . . . Let compassion sustain your houses, if you wish that your posterity be not buried under their ruins."3

Massillon was not merely an abstract dreamer preaching vague, utopian hopes. Centuries before any nation had a graduated income tax, he called upon the rich to voluntarily set aside a percentage of their income for the poor:

> If each of you were, according to the advice of the apostle, to appropriate a certain portion of your wealth toward the subsistence of the poor; if, in the computation of your expenses and of your revenues, this item were to be always regarded as the most sacred and the most inviolable one, then we should quickly see the number of the afflicted to diminish: we should soon see renewed in the church that peace, that happiness, and that cheerful equality which reigned among the first Christians; we should no longer behold with sorrow that monstrous disproportion, which, elevating the one places him on the pinnacle of prosperity and opulence, while the other crawls on the ground, and groans in the gulf of poverty and affliction. . . . and the enemies of the faith would again, as formerly, be forced to render glory to God, and to confess that there is something of divine in a religion which is capable of uniting men together in a manner so new.4

No wonder Massillon was not invited back to the court in the last years of the king's reign! But to everyone's astonishment, Louis designated the prophetic Massillon to preach his funeral. It was an honor lusted for by every preacher in France. (Unfortunately for the French nobility, Massillon had already preached the funeral of imperial France, though no one knew it.) His opening words at that occasion in Notre Dame cathedral were: "My friends, God alone is great."

The lesson of history is clear. If the message of prophets such as Massillon—or Martin Luther King—are not heard by the privileged of our society, their words will preside over our funerals. Our touch upon the less fortunate can be healing in many ways now. But if we don't reach out to them, their touch will be a judgment upon us later.

We don't have Jesus' gift of healing in our touch. But Jesus himself said that believers will do "greater works than these" (John 14:12). Around the world, the touch of Jesus through the hands of his followers has healed many a broken spirit and suffering body. To give food to the hungry in the Sudan is a touch that heals. To dig wells for villages in Nigeria is a touch that heals. To fix abscessed teeth in Central America is a touch that heals. To provide shelter for abused women in the cities of this country is a touch that heals.

In our modern society, touch can no longer mean merely one neighbor going next door to help bring in the crops or comfort a grieving family. That next-door neighborly touch must go on, of course. The person at our gate is still our personal responsibility. But if our vision only extends next door, we won't do the work of Christ. After all, these days all you have to do to avoid poor Lazarus is move into one of our elegant, restricted subdivisions with a guard at the gate. If ulcer-ridden Lazarus and his friends don't have an owner's pass on the windshield of their broken-down pickup, they'll never get inside in the first place. We must reach out through all the bars of social and economic barriers to touch the world's needy at our gates.

Remember, too, that Jesus promised the kingdom to the little people, not the rich people. His own disciples didn't understand that, and they were with him every day. No wonder the church today has such a problem with it. No rabbi in the first century would allow women, much less children, to attend his teaching. The disciples were quick to see the wisdom of that practice. After all, if children could hang around Jesus, how would they get men to take him seriously? The apostles forgot that Jesus referred to them, too, as "little children." It must have come as a thunderbolt the day Jesus embraced a child they had pushed away and then fired this warning shot across their bows: "Unless you become like children, you will never enter the kingdom of heaven" (Matt 18:3). Allen Boesak, a noted South African preacher, commented on this childlike attitude as it relates to the Kingdom:

> If Jesus promises the kingdom to these children who are blocked by the disciples for precisely this reason—after all, on what grounds do they have the right to see the master?—he does not do

it on the basis of any special quality that these children possess: childlike simplicity, trust, innocence, or open-mindedness. On the contrary, he makes it known that the kingdom of God is destined for the nobodies, the despised, the unimportant ones!

And herein lies the proof of the radicalism of the kingdom of God. The Messiah makes it plain that his realm is not intended for the prominent, the rich, the status-holders, the powerful; no, quite the reverse! What verse 15 says is: those who do not grasp this truth and take it to heart and govern their lives in accordance with it shall not enter the kingdom of God.

This nettling attitude of Jesus has not been digested by the church even today. And the antics performed to circumvent it are strange to behold. Then as now, this attitude of the Messiah (which incidentally, is maintained consistently throughout the whole Bible) stands at odds not only with what the "world" wants, but also with what the church wants![5]

The Church: Touching or Glad-Handing?

What does the church today want? A church full of nobodies, those nobody else recruits? Or the influential and prestigious? Can any institution, including the church, resist the temptation to preach what the well-to-do want to hear, to vote as the wealthy expect it to vote? Can the church's ministers resist back-slapping the wealthiest and stiff-arming the poorest, even if indirectly?

Once when I was the pastor of a church in North Louisiana, a knock on the outside door of my study interrupted my sermon preparation. The slight woman who came in was a stranger to me. She said she wasn't a church member; she had just knocked on my study door because she needed somebody to talk to. Her first son had died of a rare blood disease three years before. She had just learned that her only other child had the same disease.

"He is only ten years-old," she said. She sat quietly crying. "I just can't give this one up, too." After a moment I asked where she lived. "Right there," she said. "Right where?" I asked. She got up. "Right there," pointing out my window, "just across the street." She pointed at an old frame house directly opposite my study. I asked how long she had lived there. "A long time. Eleven years." She looked embarrassed. "I know I should have come to the church before this."

Touch

The next Sunday I chided the deacons at their monthly meeting for not telling me that the new vice-president at the glass plant was a Baptist. Three men spoke at once. "We did tell you! We told you last week!" "I know you did," I said. "You always tell me when the new manager of Penney's is a Baptist, or an incoming professor or dean at the college. But nobody told me about the lady across the street who's lost one son already and is about to lose her other son." They looked pained, those who knew what I was talking about. The others looked confused or angry. "It's not your fault," I told them. "It's mine. It's ours, the church's. We are alert to anyone who can help us. We're sometimes blind, or indifferent, to those who just need our help."

It's not a pretty sight, the go-getter church of today; careful not to brush the kitty of culture the wrong way, and increasingly unlikely to bring home the sick and hungry creatures the world looks at as strays. Even if it did, it wouldn't be enough. We can't do it all, even if we would. There are too many of them and too few of us—all of us, even all the churches. Our touch can no longer be direct in every case. Like it or not, our touch will have to be used to provoke the secular rulers to works of righteousness. Only a nation as a whole can heal hurts.

Many Christians are more afraid of "government control" than they are of neglecting the hurting part of society Jesus ministered to and lived with. A volunteer fire department is better than nothing, especially in small, rural towns. But a volunteer fire department system in Chicago or Los Angeles would be a catastrophe. Are professional fire departments a form of creeping socialism? Heard anyone say lately about the fire department: "Why don't we do it through the churches?" Unless reasonable thinking in our nation prevails about the human needs around us, our society is going back to frontier days in its care for hungry, neglected, and abused children; the sick elderly; and the mentally ill.

The touch of the church today means voting right, being sure that organized selfishness is not allowed to run the country. It means reaching across state and national lines to share our abundance with those children of God who live far from us but are near to the heart of God. Anything less is to ignore the inclusiveness of the touch of Jesus.

Perhaps the reason many of us in the church have a hard time being sympathetic with indirect, more global touching of the needy is because we have never known the joy of personally touching the needs of the world. That kind of caring touch, whether near or far, brings a rare inspiration to these last, weary days of the twentieth century. Mary Cosby of the Church of the Saviour in Washington tells of the joy that comes to the one who reaches out to others:

> One of the mission groups of the Church of the Saviour—the Ministry of Money—uses the phrase reverse mission to describe how much North Americans receive when they give to the Third World. Several times each year, opportunity is given to both middle class and poor people to travel to Calcutta, Haiti, Africa, or Central America to be with people in some of the world's most troubled places of the earth. Ken Morton, a biochemist from Detroit, went to Calcutta and experienced more joy than ever before. He tells of feeding a withered, broken old man with a gray, stubby beard who was too weak to sit up. Accidentally he spilled a few grains of rice onto the old man's neck. At first he left the rice there because he did not want to risk touching him. But after some time, he realized that the rice was probably uncomfortable and that he should remove it.
>
> "As soon as I touched him, all heaven broke loose," Morton remembers. "He began to speak, smile and wiggle his head in that peculiar Indian way. Though I couldn't understand his words, the body language was unmistakable: he was overwhelmed with the simple joy of a kind, human touch. . . . At some point during this time something surprising happened to me. A big, childish irrepressible grin came over my face. I had become infected with his joy. It was a joy so deep that I had almost forgotten that such feelings even existed. Joy just seemed to flow between us as we looked at each other."
>
> "Then thoughts began to come to me," Morton concludes. "I realized that up until this point my reading, thinking, and experiencing of Calcutta had focused on the suffering of the poor and on the identification of Jesus (and ourselves) with their suffering. But here I was being confronted with an experience of pure joy that seemed to contradict all of that. If indeed I had met Jesus in this man, then I had met not only the suffering Jesus, but also the Jesus of great joy."[6]

Could it be that the recovery of joy in our frantic, pressured, and often gray world—"A joy so deep I had almost forgotten such feelings even existed"—waits upon our risking to touch someone who needs us? Could it be that another of the strange sayings of Jesus, "It is more blessed to give than to receive," nowadays generally regarded as a joke, is a basic truth of existence? Is it possible that in fact it is we who are the beggars at life's gate, and that the touch we withhold from others is in fact the wondrous touch of the fairy tale that would turn our own leaden lives into gold?

On the Sunday morning Samuel Proctor was to be installed as pastor of the Abyssinian Baptist Church in New York, he stood at the back of the church in an elegant robe, surrounded by the church choir, waiting to begin the processional to the platform. A huge crowd filled the church to overflowing. About halfway down the center aisle, a child stood at the end of one row. He was partly out into the aisle. Proctor noticed that the boy was looking back at him, his eyes wide, his mouth open in wonder. The child had Down's Syndrome. As the organ began its triumphant music, Proctor led the singing procession down the aisle. When he reached the boy, who was now gazing straight up at the pastor, he paused briefly, smiled at the boy, and winked, then plunked him on the top of his head with his thumb and index finger. For a second the boy was confused. But when he saw the twinkle in Proctor's eyes, he suddenly broke into a wide grin and turned eagerly toward his parents to let them know something wonderful had happened.

Every Sunday after that, the boy was in the same place, always smiling as he looked back toward his friend, always waiting expectantly for the funny tap on his head. Proctor said, "Nobody ever taught me the theology of head plunking. Sometimes you've just got to know when a sacerdotal plunk on the head is the right thing to do."

No, Sam, there you're wrong. Somebody did teach you. Somebody a long time ago, who also knew the magic of a touch. Somebody who, if he had been there himself, would have given the boy the same smile and wink, and a sacerdotal plunk on the top of his head. That same somebody wants us all to share the gift of touch with those who are dying to receive it.

Walter Bruggemann quotes a "hopeless, homeless woman" from Jonathan Kozol's book, *Rachel and Her Children: Homeless Families in America*, on the God whose touch is merciful:

> The Bible is what taught me to read. When I read those "thee's and thou's," I have this dream. God comes to me. He calls me "thee." I call him "Thou."[7]

Notes

[1] *USA Today*, February 16, 1993.

[2] Robert Coles, *Harvard Diary: Reflections on the Sacred and the Secular* (New York: Crossroads, 1988) 203.

[3] Clyde E. Fant, Jr. and William M. Pinson, Jr., *Twenty Centuries of Great Preaching*, 13 vols. (Waco TX: Word Publishing, 1971)2: 390.

[4] Ibid., 391.

[5] Allen Boesak, "Presence of the Hidden God," *The Finger of God* (Maryknoll NY: Orbis Books, 1982) 71-72.

[6] Mary Crosby, "Called to Intimacy, Called to Mission: The Inward Journey," *Christian Ministry* 17, no. 6 (November 1986): 12-13.

[7] Walter Brueggemann, *Finally Comes the Poet* (Minneapolis: Fortress Press, 1989) 148.